# PRAISE FOR
## *JOURNEY BETWEEN TWO WORLDS*

"*Journey Between Two Worlds* is a moving chronicle of hardship, hope, and renewal. Karola Schuette recounts her remarkable experiences with vivid details, engaging humor, and, above all, unflagging courage."

—**Christopher Porterfield,** Retired Executive Editor,
*TIME Magazine*

"A delicate mosaic of daily-life detail . . . gives us humble insight into . . . world-historical events. . . . From these modest, private writings comes a masterful picture of the twentieth century. . . . An impressively moving read."

—**Professor Marcia Pally,** NYU, Humboldt University-Berlin, Author of *From This Broken Hill I Sing to You: God, Sex, and Politics in the Work of Leonard Cohen*

"*Journey Between Two Worlds* is a charming, evocative story illustrating the experiences faced by a brave, young German woman. . . . Karola's voice is loud and clear, and her passionate devotion to her husband, family, and new country is vividly illuminated."

—**Cynde Bloom Lahey,** Director of Library Information Services, Norwalk Public Library, CT

*Journey Between Two Worlds*

by Karola M. Schuette

© Copyright 2021 Karola M. Schuette

ISBN 978-1-64663-353-1

Published by

 köehlerbooks™

3705 Shore Drive
Virginia Beach, VA 23455
800-435-4811
www.koehlerbooks.com

# JOURNEY BETWEEN TWO WORLDS

KAROLA M. SCHUETTE

VIRGINIA BEACH
CAPE CHARLES

*To My Love, Bill,*
*who changed my life forever.*

# TABLE OF CONTENTS

# INTRODUCTION

**FOR YEARS WE CHILDREN WOULD** hear our mother, Karola, recount bits and pieces of her upbringing during the Great Depression and war years in Germany. How otherworldly and remote much of it sounded to our innocent American ears. As we grew older and learned more about life, it became clear that her memories should be preserved in a lasting form instead of relying on our own recollections. The drama in her experiences could not be made up or disputed; her memories were of personal and historic significance and deserved to be passed on. That was how *Journey Between Two Worlds* began.

Though writing was not foreign to Karola, this was different. She launched into her memoir during the years following our father Bill's passing in 1986. His absence reminded her that she could no longer ask her deceased German relatives the curious, burning questions about them that surfaced in her mind. She wanted to spare us that burden. Gathering her thoughts, feelings, and remembrances in written form would serve to convey her inner life and engender a sense of intimate connection. We would not be left wondering what Karola thought or felt.

Her writing process for *Journey Between Two Worlds* was by no means linear. Karola would produce a series of individual topic pages in fits and starts over the course of about ten years, originating on a word processor. At the completion of each rough draft, she sent copies to all her children, soliciting a response and commentary.

Encouraged by her family and close friends, Karola submitted further pages when she could muster the emotional fortitude to relive a particular memory. She would refer to the developing work as her *saga, my story*, or *the book*, with the intention of creating a legacy for her loved ones.

Along with the text, Karola augmented her story with copies of an extensive cache of saved documents and photos. How amazing that she still had so many of those! Ultimately each of her children and two grandchildren received a three-ring binder containing her unedited words, related images and documents, and any additional information specific to each of us. The result was what could more accurately be described as a memoir scrapbook. Organization was Karola's middle name.

Normally, this could well have culminated the endeavor. But no. With increasing encouragement from her close circle, Karola wanted to press further toward publishing. She longed to see her story between "two real covers." After much contemplation she arrived at the title *Journey Between Two Worlds*. She visualized the cover and developed a more ordered structure—all before a hint of any publishing resource was in sight. As health issues began to intervene, Karola became restless about time. She had hoped that all would be completed by her ninetieth birthday in December 2012. But not yet, so onward she trekked. Karola succumbed to illness in June of 2013, though not before she was promised that her publication dream would be fulfilled.

And now, after eight additional years, *Journey Between Two*

*Worlds* has expanded from the private domain of our three-ring binders to the distinctive public embrace of "two real covers."

✳ ✳ ✳

My process of editing *Journey Between Two Worlds* has been akin to a continuing visit with my mother. Each time I read her words I hear her voice and feel the warmth of our conversational exchanges. It is reassuring and uplifting. With all the hardship she lived through, it is inspiring how optimistic she remained. Her fearless attitude and generosity of spirit, combined with her unwavering love, serve as a guiding light. It is an honor to make Karola's *Journey Between Two Worlds* available to a wider audience of readers so that they, too, may have the opportunity to share a visit with her. For those who take the journey, Karola and her story are a perpetual gift.

Margaret Schuette<br>Editor

# CHAPTER 1

## *My Inspiration*

**I WOULD NOT HAVE MUCH** of a story to tell if it were not for the arrival in Germany of a German-born American soldier named William Hermann Schuette. Up until then I did not feel my life had been of interest to anybody. World War II, with all its tyranny, had come to an end but destruction, desolation, and hunger, combined with hopelessness, was all around. In early October 1946, William Schuette entered the scene.

He wrote this account in his diary:

> In the spring of 1946, I looked forward with anxiety to being discharged from the army, not because I had any complaints about my work or conditions, but rather the desire for a change. My work in the service was highly educational and interesting to me. The great majority of the boys were quite intellectual and generally good company and the recreational facilities unlimited. I shall never forget the wonderful times I had in Washington, DC on the Potomac River and at Jiggs. I left the army on April 28. At that time, I had an agreement

with the Contingency Program Management Office to work in Frankfurt, Germany for Colonel Wentworth within three weeks. Due to circumstances this fell through; several weeks passed, however, before I found out about it. During the five summer months of leisure, I did paintings, read the classics, played accordion, cards, and chess; most days were spent on the beach. I was very happy to hear I was to leave the States on September 26 aboard the *SS George Washington* for Bremerhaven, Germany to accept a job at the Civil Censorship Division (CCD) in Frankfurt, Germany. This was an opportunity to see Germany again and at the same time save a little money while employed as a War Department Employee (WDE) in the American occupied zone.

The voyage was very pleasant, lively, and educational for me. I understand that the *SS George Washington* as an army transport ship could carry as many as 6,000 men, whereas we were only 1,000. Arriving in Bremerhaven on October 6, nothing much of interest was to be seen until we boarded the train for Frankfurt the following day. Passing through the cities of Hannover and Kassel one could see the devastation along the journey and notice the frail, bewildered condition of the people. US vehicles and men in uniform (occupational forces) were at all important points. My biggest surprise came when I saw Frankfurt. Here it seemed that every building was damaged in one way or another. The rare undamaged ones provided lodging for Allied personnel. Where the hundreds of thousands of people actually lived, I didn't know. Strangely enough, instead of sympathizing with these poor, ragged, and hungry individuals, one became hardened and indifferent to all the misery. I felt a little uneasy at this point of my life being back in Germany, now destroyed beyond recognition, and wondered what the village of my birth may at this time look like and what the people there must have suffered. Eventually I would see for myself.

Doing a quick survey of the type of work I was about to undertake, I found that some of it was more or less negligible. There we were in CCD checking everyone and anything that a German writes or talks about, and even arresting quite a number of CIC (Civilian Identity Certification), whom we in this branch still considered dangerous. The general atmosphere was tense, and suspicion constantly kept one on guard. No one knew who was enemy, spy, or to be trusted. On a daily basis I was transported from my living quarters (a shared apartment with other WDEs) in a compound in the town of Offenbach to Frankfurt, where my actual assignment was to censor telegrams and phone calls going in and out of the American occupied zone.

William Schuette, Army Intelligence officer

The Offenbach compound had within its confines our living quarters, a mess hall, and a PX (post exchange), where all personnel could buy their rations and other available goods not accessible anywhere else. The compound was fenced in by high security fences, had guards at all points, and included the motor pool. Below, in the basement, were long tables where German men and women (carefully screened for their character and aptitude and sworn to maintain absolute secrecy about their work) opened, read, censored, and then sealed again all mail leaving the occupied zone. They also went through the very same process with incoming mail from the other occupied zones within Germany, so the recipient in many cases could ultimately not make sense of the letter's censored contents. Everyone had to be checked entering or leaving the compound. The Germans not only had to show their identification but also wear yellow buttons. Any sign of suspicious appearance caused a body search; all kinds of food were the most common items smuggled.

There was also an office called Special Services where one could buy the military publication *Stars and Stripes*, rent a bike that was shipped over from the States, and get a ticket to a movie, the theater or Saturday night dance. The latter, which were held in makeshift or hurriedly repaired quarters, were provided as a welcome distraction to get away from the depressing daily picture: ruined landscapes, buildings, and the general spy atmosphere on the outside.

In this Special Services office worked a young woman whom I immediately took great interest in and found very attractive. But with my work schedule I did not find a chance to even talk to her, other than office talk, since she was also constantly observed by supervisors so as not to get personal or friendly with anyone. But I knew then and there already that I would ask to come to her house sometime and hoped this would be soon. She would not get out of my mind. Maybe I could ask to visit for a holiday. I felt a great love for her and knew for sure we would be married.

circa 1942 Karola

In the next visit to the Special Services office (under the guise of wanting to buy a theater ticket), I wished to find out more about her and, under some official excuse, said I needed to see her building pass. I had guessed her age to be about nineteen and could hardly believe that she was to be twenty-four on December 29 that year. I was hoping somehow to wangle an invitation for Christmas, just to get things going, but it took another long week before I finally was invited to her place for Christmas Eve.

*❋ ❋ ❋*

Here I have to take over from Bill with my own recollections.

I had come to work in this Civil Censorship Division via a long employment preparation. After finishing eight years of school at age fourteen, I became a legal secretary-apprentice at a lawyer's office for the summer of 1937, attending evening courses in stenography, typing, and bookkeeping. The lawyer was transferred out of Offenbach to someplace near the Rhein, which made my three-year learning contract null and void. However, he was able to find me another firm in the same building, where I continued my contract until an appropriate office was secured for me to accomplish my legal secretary training. Bill collection firm Bien was sort of slave labor for me. I had to be there by seven o'clock, an hour before anyone else, and my duties included cleaning the potbelly stove, carrying out the ashes to the garbage, starting a new fire, and fetching water for a hot beverage to accommodate the other four employees and owners. In addition, dusting the office was a necessity, along with sharpening pencils and putting new ribbons in the outdated typewriters. By this time the place was beginning to warm up. I needed to wash my dirty hands and put on a white office coat to set myself apart as the underling apprentice. In one way the coat came in handy. It covered up my totally poor wardrobe. Then, around nine, everybody would give a list of what they wanted to eat for breakfast. It always meant a trip to the bakery for warm *Broetchen* (rolls), then to the butcher for hot breakfast sausage, fresh from a steaming kettle. Everyone, of course, wanted something different. One could say I served my apprenticeship in *office management and breakfast assembling technology* before I was even allowed to sit at a typewriter to type up warning letters to people with overdue bills. There was the starter, appropriately called the Number One letter, and then they went all the way to fire-alarm-police-whistle-sharp Number Ten! What happened after the tenth letter? I was not allowed to find out, and in any case, I had been sworn to secrecy.

After a few months with the Bien firm, I could at last continue my apprenticeship with a genuine established lawyer, a wonderful person named Dr. Goebel. Now my real training began. I was still doing the breakfast run, but everything was on a much more refined level. I did filing, brought my employer's robe to the courthouse, and often was trusted to deliver a client's file. Finally came the big moments of taking shorthand and typing the letters or court files myself. Many of those called for carbon copies, sometimes as many as five or six. The tragedy was in making a typing error. To erase the mistake one could only erase the top page after a tiny piece of paper was carefully inserted underneath each carbon paper on the very spot, a most time-consuming and irritating process. The copies that were on much thinner paper would usually reveal a smudge, no matter how carefully they were corrected. Such was the beginner's lot.

During the years preceding my first taste of employment, while I was still a student, Hitler had become the new messiah for his party. Bit by bit he had charmed Germany's youth into his ideology and created job opportunities for those suffering unemployment. Among them was my father, who had been unemployed for as long as I could remember. Finally, he got a job applying his training as a *Maschinenschlosser* (machinist), and simultaneously I was hired into apprenticeship as a future legal secretary. My mother could not believe that after all the miserable years of stretching one Deutsche Mark for a day, we could eat more nourishing food, as well as buy much needed new linen. It was like Christmas, until my father came home from his first day of work, quite shattered about the kinds of things that were now being built. The firm of Hartmann, known as a reputable manufacturer, was now making parts for the war machine, as my father would say. Hitler was beginning to rattle his saber; therefore, it wouldn't be long before that machinery was put to use. What a sobering, scary discovery this was for him. We paid attention to my father's words, although he was known as quite a pessimist. We did pay attention. Since the Hitler party by now had most everything in its vise-like grip, one had to stand at attention, salute at attention, and practically never lose attention. Every official or business letter had to be signed with *Heil Hitler*. Beware of forgetting this requirement, or you were put under surveillance. *Beware, beware. You are suspect.*

I have to mention these things because they tied in with every aspect of existence: your daily life, your religious beliefs, your relationship with friends and family, every detail of your waking hours. It culminated in not trusting your own self in your sleep. A neighbor might hear something, denounce you to the authorities to make points with the party, and have you deported to a labor camp. Even in school religious instruction with a Protestant minister and a Catholic priest, each teaching two hours a week, was eliminated and replaced with sports. All of a sudden, our Jewish friends did not attend public school anymore. The word was they were being taught in the synagogue. Slowly it became obvious one could no longer patronize Jewish stores. They were taken over by Aryan establishments. We were constantly under scrutiny because of our Jewish sounding name of Friedmann, and we had to produce umpteen documents verifying our ancestry. The age of persecution had begun. The meaning of trust, friendship, and caring about, or for, another human being felt forever buried under tons of cement. Forget about love. It was never openly demonstrated before, but now any dream of love for another person, or even for God, had to be completely removed from your mind.

About the time the Jewish students seemed banned from public school, each teacher was pressured to join the party. In fact, the entire faculty was coerced into joining as one body. It was obvious that refusal meant losing the job for a lifetime, along with being placed on a permanent blacklist. Once the teachers were all party members, they had to see to it that their students joined the Hitler Youth. The teachers had to keep strict lists as to who had joined and who had not. The younger children were an easier target for promoting enthusiasm to join. For them being a member meant fun activities: marching and singing rallies, being in uniform, and feeling important, many for the first time in their lives.

I had a sad but handy excuse for not having to join the Youth: I needed to assist my mother. From the time of my birth, she had been ailing with varicose veins that over time became ulcerated. Eventually, I received a permanent written dispensation from my mother's physician, Dr. Baehr. He was her doctor for years—a miracle worker. I will never forget his kindness in treating her many times when the socialized system blocked her from medical attention, since we didn't have any money to repay even the smallest fee. My mother's poor health became my escape from all this Party madness. I could stay home and be of help. It went without saying, however, that as an only child, and a daughter at that, I led a very isolated life. Once, when we went for an appointment at Dr. Baehr's office, we got the shock of our lives. We learned that he had suddenly left on a long vacation, his return uncertain. In fact, his entire family had left. His nurse mentioned that, just in case, he had referred us to another family doctor in town. She herself was to look for other employment. We realized we had been the patients of a Jewish doctor. It was now certain in our minds that he would never return. We hoped he had left under his own dictates, quietly, overnight, leaving everything behind and exiting to England, France, or Switzerland. One could not discuss his disappearance with anyone for fear of the looming unknown ahead for all of us. We realized how brutally our entire world was changing, like an unstoppable rollercoaster, going down, down. The web was being pulled tighter and we had become puppet prisoners with no escape in sight. People with foreign connections and money could still leave, but for the rest of us there was no way out. Bonfires were lit, burning volumes of books by Jewish authors. Music by Jewish composers was no longer being played. History books were rewritten with student curriculums being *Hitlerized*. Suddenly you could be a struggling, deficient student, but as long as you knew Hitler's birthdate, you got a passing grade. Was this possible? Yes, it became possible. But, no, do not criticize nor let your face betray your thoughts; the enemy suddenly could be anybody. This insanity had no end and the *Marschmusik* played on and on and on.

It seemed like my cousins Rudi and Karl, who were several years older than I, had just been confirmed in the *Schlosskirche* (Castle Church) in Offenbach. Now they were being drafted into the *Reichsarbeitsdienst* (RAD, the German government youth workforce). It meant that they had to interrupt the apprenticeship contracts just extended to them and serve in this category of pre-army duty. They wore uniforms and were trained in camps, drilled like any aspiring soldier, only these groups were building Hitler's *Autobahnen* (motorways). They were committed to this arrangement for at least half a year, and in some cases an entire year. After discharging their duty, the draftees were allowed to return to their former apprenticeships. Later, many pursued similar construction work as a career.

With all this recruiting going on, teachers were required to distribute, on a trial basis, ration coupons for certain food staples. Again, how clever to involve the teachers, as they had a highly respected standing in their communities. Since teachers were doing the distribution, few people would object to or resist this regulation. And the teachers' response? Well, they had to hold onto their jobs for their families. With the overall employment situation improving by leaps and bounds, suddenly Hitler began preaching that the German *Volk* (people) needed more

*Lebensraum* (space for the growing population). He became persistent about expanding towards the east, meaning toward Poland. As a result, I heard over the radio September 1, 1939 that our troops had marched into Poland. It was so shocking to me. At that moment it hit me that life as we had known it was undergoing a radical change and would never be the same again. The big unknown had now become a deeply dark and menacing threat. Air raid sirens were installed on rooftops on every block and tests began, just so we would be *protected*. From what, I wondered. Poland was surely far away. And what had the Polish people done to us? Every few blocks huge building projects began to take shape with meters-thick concrete walls, reinforced with the strongest steel. What these buildings were to be no one knew, least of all the folks working there. It was generally assumed that they were for grain and food storage. On all the kiosks, formerly covered only with advertisements for consumer goods (and always pitching party slogans), large signs now appeared: *Psst, the enemy is listening in!* In other words, beware of whatever you talk about, as there is no trust possible anymore. Think about that.

By that time, I had reached the end of my third year in apprenticeship and could soon look forward to receiving a higher salary, but it was not to be. I was ordered to report for recruitment into the female version of *Reichsarbeitsdienst* (RAD) or forfeit my job. If I was physically fit, I would then become a work maid, helping the farmers whose sons were now marching into Poland and who knows where else.

The time was also drawing near when I could expect my own draft notice, since my eighteenth birthday was approaching. The draft into the *Reichsarbeitsdienst* came early in spring in the form of a postcard. One *had* to appear or else there was no hope of going back to one's former job, or any job for that matter. Your name would be placed on the blacklist until doomsday. I passed the physical exam, in which it was established that I was blood type O. Later, I learned that all females with blood type O would be detailed to join up with selected young men to further the Aryan race, in effect creating baby farms. My God! I escaped this fate through sheer luck. An infection under two nails on my left hand put me on the sick list near the end of my service time, so I was dismissed. What a happy disgrace. But I'm jumping ahead of myself.

Wherever I would be placed was to appear on the travel notice. I strongly hoped to go somewhere away from air raid alarms and food and clothing shortages. After all, Hitler had to feed and clothe this army that was to help the farmers! The travel notice came in military form. I departed from Frankfurt Station on a long train heading south, stopping here and there for more recruits. By evening we had reached Munich. Because of a miscalculation, no further trains were available to reach our destination of Neumarkt am Wallersee in Austria, which now belonged to Germany under Hitler. We had to sleep in the Munich Station with no blankets and no hot food. The next morning we were a miserable lot. We were herded like cattle into separate local trains. We were thrown together with all kinds of Bavarian and Austrian dialect-speaking, stinking-cheese-eating people staring at us like we had arrived from another planet. We had to work for them? Lord help us. Hopefully we would not have to fight our own war now just to be understood, or to comprehend what one another was saying. It was truly like we came from another world.

That afternoon, after many more stops of unloading girls at different camps, we arrived at our camp. The barracks were located in a little valley. We had to hike to them from the station despite all having blisters on our feet. I can say we also had arrived at full-blown culture shock combined with bone-deep fatigue. But there was no rest for the weary. We were assigned our lockers, bunk beds, sheets, uniforms, instructions for lights-out call and early flag-call, which meant that we all had to be on the double in a circle around the flag mast, singing a military marching song, doing the Hitler salute while one of the leaders raised the flag. It was the same drill in the evening, flag-down with all possible pomp and circumstance, regardless of wind or weather.

✳ ✳ ✳

1947 Bill's love letter

Letter from Bill to Karola, translated from the original German:

January 1947

My Darling Karola,

As you probably know, I am not a great friend of writing (which I probably inherited from my father), but today I will try and write you in my native language. In this short time since we have known each other, I have lived very happy days with you. It seems that we have known one another for years already, and it is really only weeks! And the more I see you, the more I love you. Today, I feel a little lonesome, but my thoughts are with you, which make me always so happy.

Your letters, I read them always with great interest and hold them in the highest esteem, so much so that I will safe-keep some of them for the rest of my life. I know that I cannot always follow my wishes as I desire, as the present time has no space for that, but through love much can be accomplished.

Now I am already being disturbed again, so that I can maybe continue tomorrow. *Na ja, so geht's* (Well, that's how it goes).

✳ ✳ ✳

It is now August 2007. I came across this letter a little while ago and had to frame it so it can send me that love every time I look at or pass by it. I am sure that Bill must have spent a few hours writing the letter, not only choosing his words but also remembering the exact penmanship style we all had to learn and write as children in those early days at school. The translation was finally done at a schoolhouse in New Canaan, Connecticut, where I now live. Imagine that.

For some strange reason, the letter reminded me of the time my three daughters and I were present in Bargfeld, Germany for Heinz and Friedhilde's forty-fifth wedding anniversary. She told the story of a special letter of her own. During their courtship—while Heinz, Bill's cousin, was waiting for Friedhilde's answer—she kind of stalled and said she would make up her mind after he wrote her a letter. She wanted to see how he could express his feelings in writing, with his penmanship, grammar, etc. I thought that was so cute and clever. Anyway, he passed the test. He had forgotten all about that letter. He looked at Friedhilde with great surprise that she had kept the letter for so long. He was very touched that she held everyone in such spellbound attention, considering he was usually the one who grabbed it all.

# CHAPTER 2

### *Christmas 1946*

**IT WAS THE FALL OF** 1946. At the time I was working for the Allied Division of the Office of Censorship in a compound located in Offenbach. The Division was housed in a few blocks of homes where Offenbach citizens formerly lived; they had to evacuate within a few hours' notice right after the American Army occupation and take only a few personal belongings. The main building within the compound had contained the offices of one of the German general insurance companies. The contents of the offices were thrown out into the street and destroyed, and a strong barbed-wire fence was immediately erected. MPs stood guard at the entrance. No one could get past them except with valid ID.

The Division's responsibility was to censor all mail and telegrams circulating among the four occupied zones within what remained of Germany. Within the compound I had the job of translating between German personnel and the Americans whenever needed. For the rest of the time I was assigned to maintain and supervise the Department of Special Services. That meant organizing transportation for weekend sightseeing to parts of the neighborhood that were not totally destroyed; arranging for tickets to American movie shows; and most enjoyable, monitoring admissions at the ticket booth at Saturday night dances, intended for the Allied personnel and their friends from nearby Frankfurt. I was especially thrilled to be the attendant at the door because of the fringe benefits that came with the assignment, like terrific American ice cream, soda, coffee, and cake, all of which I asked to be saved until the dance was over. I could then take them home to my parents, who had neither seen nor eaten such treats for the last six years. After the dance started, I had to retire to a back room because, after all, I was still *the former enemy* (and sometimes not so former). But I did not mind, since all that really counted was the food. This job paid a monthly salary in German script money and it, too, was minor. The biggest compensation was a hot lunch (whatever the daily menu), plus two slices of bread with a thick slice of Spam. I would eat the hot lunch, but the bread and Spam were kept for my parents. They were waiting eagerly for it when I came home in the afternoon.

Toward the end of November, the previous Allied personnel were rotated home and replaced by a fresh crew from the United States. Whenever I entered the main gate during the following weeks, one of them passed me on the way out toward a waiting truck for work in the Frankfurt Censorship Division. He always gave me the once-over, accompanied by a hurried "hello." Next thing I knew, he would appear in my office, always wanting some information, a roll of string, a newspaper—all just excuses to start a conversation. Then, once when we were about to pass each other in a hallway, he quickly asked me if he could visit me at home. This cost him some nerve, since open fraternization at that time was not yet tolerated. I thought he was surely a brazen fellow because these incidents happened now on a daily basis. I had to think of excuses to stop this nonsense. When I discussed the matter with one of the other German secretaries, she said, "Next time he asks you just tell him how dilapidated your circumstances are at home, and if this does not discourage him, invite him. This is the only way to find out what he is all about."

So, when the next time came I told him we lived in a war-damaged apartment with boarded up windows, makeshift furniture, a primitive stove, but no heating material, and we would go to bed early just to stay reasonably warm. And we had nothing to offer in the way of food! Nothing seemed to turn him off. He invited himself for Christmas, so I asked my parents and it was fine with them. We were all in a suspenseful state. How was this going to work out? We felt that we had nothing to lose and he would be the one to be bitterly disappointed. The only certain thing I had found out about him was that he originally was born in Germany and still had relatives up north in the British occupied zone. The Germany he remembered was the one he left as an eleven-year-old boy with his younger brother, sister, and his mother to join their father, who had preceded them by six months to America to make a new and better life.

The morning of the twenty-fourth came, and with it a taxi with this fellow unloading and schlepping canned and other goods like Danish pastries, bacon, butter, salami, mayonnaise, bread, rolls, coffee, a coffee pot, can opener, apples, oranges, nuts, chocolate, Lifesavers, a cardboard box of firewood and briquets, and matches. It was as if a fairy godmother had used her magic wand. He did all of this in a hurry so that the neighbors would not be wise to it. He had to make another haul and come back later in the day! The very man who had been so persistent in wanting to come as our guest now showered us with gifts. Now we felt quite overcome by his massive generosity. Dawning on us also was the fact that he had sacrificed all his ration points, no doubt having saved them up for weeks in advance and exchanged the rest for cigarettes on the black market. And he was coming back later in the day? With more? Or what? Was this his shy way of giving us the present of sustenance?

Late afternoon, almost at dusk, there was that taxi again. What excitement, such as I could not remember ever. There was Bill, this time carrying a small Christmas tree from the nearby woods, an accordion, and a pillowcase full of wrapped assorted boxes. He made a fire in the small living room stove, leaned the tree in the opposite corner, and broke open the Lifesavers. They served as tree ornaments, edible too, and the man had even brought tinsel from somewhere. My mother was crying, my father was speechless, and we were all on an emotional roller coaster. This was a thawing out from the previous years of war, deprivation, and hopelessness. We had never had genuine coffee, even before the war, and we were at a loss how to boil it, so Bill came to the rescue. There was apparently no end to this man's magic.

I do not remember if we had anything like a main meal. It was more like a sampling of everything plus a bottle of wine to rinse things down. He had even thought of the corkscrew. When Bill found out there was a lonesome single mother with a six-year-old daughter living in hiding upstairs, he asked them down to join us. Little Brigitte had never seen an orange or chocolate. We all had a feast that reached our stomachs, but more profoundly, our hearts. My father received cigarettes, cigars, and socks, and my mother fancy handkerchiefs, cologne, and great smelling soap— luxury items we hadn't been able to cherish in years! For me there were stockings, a beautiful music box, and finely embroidered handkerchiefs. It was like a dream.

Then this wonder of a man pulled out his accordion and we were supposed to sing *Stille Nacht* (*Silent Night*). I had not heard my father sing since I was a little child when we went hiking in the woods, nor did I remember my mother ever singing. I had not done anything of this sort since leaving school. Under Herr Hitler it was frowned upon anyway, a weak sort of thing to do, other than the rally and marching songs. Brigitte did not have any inkling of what a Christmas song was like.

The accordion and Bill led us into *Stille Nacht*. The sounds, smells, and warmth of what Christmas was a long time ago made us feel aglow (the wine helped a little too). We could blame it on the alcohol when our eyes brimmed over. It did not matter if everybody saw it because we all were under the same spell. We felt a little ashamed not remembering the second, third, and remaining verses of this lovely song. The war had buried all of it and made us like robots. Yet here was this man who left as a child, lived in America so many years, came back, and remembered. We recognized what had become of us at that instant. But the beautiful reality was that we could go back to our childhood, to our enchantment, to our songs.

I did not want this evening to end. The fire in the stove had burned down. Brigitte had to go upstairs and be put to bed. My parents did not know how to thank Bill, but then he confessed to us what a wonderful time he had and thanked us all for letting him spend Christmas Eve with us. Without hesitation he asked my parents if he might come back to visit, maybe on New Year's Eve. They were lost for an answer; they did not want to give the impression that we welcomed him only for all the goods he might bring, so they simply said, "We'll see."

I put my coat on and accompanied the now empty-handed Bill downstairs and a little ways to the park before I returned home. Bill said again what a lovely Christmas Eve it had been and he was hoping to see us again. The smart fellow had purposely forgotten his accordion at our place. Then he said something that didn't quite sink into my brain: "I am going to marry you." And with that breathless remark he hurried away.

As I turned to go back to our apartment it slowly began to snow. It felt and smelled like Christmas long ago, even outdoors. The events of this miraculous day went through my head again and again. They warmed me so much that it was not noticeable that the stove in the living room had grown cold. The warmth was the magic of Christmas as it happened in 1946.

※ ※ ※

He said he wanted to marry me? Probably that was just a matter of babbling and then forgetting. Yet he did not seem the kind of person to say something lightly and not mean it. Well, the next days and weeks would bring verification that I had not dreamt this. Bill had hit it off with my father just great, which in itself was exceptional, my father being a very critical judge of people and unbelievably jealous and afraid of losing his daughter. Watching these two men converse about various subjects and my father not flying off the handle or trying to win the upper hand was something that had just not happened before. Bill came for New Year's Eve, again with packages of food and a bottle of wine. His quiet persistence in creating a comfortable atmosphere to speak of his family background and relatives in Northern Germany was a diplomatic ploy leading to the question: "Is it alright for me to take you to my relatives in the British occupied zone in January and introduce you to them?"

I guess my parents felt too awkward to say no, so they agreed to this planned undertaking (if it was alright with me). It was up to me to say yes, even though I had not been asked yet. By intuition I felt that this man must be utterly sincere, and I knew my answer for the adventure would be yes!

Bill never wore his uniform. He always came calling in his civilian clothes, since he felt more comfortable this way anyhow. He also knew how quickly neighbors would sit in judgment over any German girl being courted by an American. Their assumption would always be the same: she is selling herself for cigarettes, these whores. The guys will just forget about them afterwards, and what a shame for the family. This is what our men fought for on the front, the girls and women to throw themselves at the enemy.

Could anybody believe in a true budding romance in these

harsh, cruel times, when all feelings of the heart were seemingly impossible, shattered by the bombs that had rained on all of us in such abundance?

I pondered these thoughts. It did not change my decision to go with Bill to his relatives. The one important factor was that when I was with Bill and he put his arms around me, never before had I felt such a sense of being loved, secure and safe against anything and anybody. I had not ever thought of myself as being lovable, or that anyone could truly care about me. It was an overwhelming feeling. Many times I would think I was just dreaming, that I would wake up and it would not be there anymore. To see Bill with some of his family would be very interesting and tell me more about this person.

1946 Bill

# CHAPTER 3

*Aboard the Train: Bill's Childhood Recollections*

**IT WAS TO BE BILL'S** first reunion with his relatives since leaving as a boy. He was coming back as an American, which also meant he was not only visiting family and former neighbors, but he was also now coming back as the winner over the former enemy. This seemed to cause mixed emotions, which would be revealed in so many roundabout remarks made by his family. The train ride from Frankfurt to Uelzen was an experience of insistent obstacles. Nobody knew what to expect at any moment. The train presented a pitiful sight. Most of the windows had been blown out by bombing raids and were boarded up. Bill wore his sloppiest looking civilian clothes and had to be careful to speak German at all times. I had no problem with looking disheveled when it counted. The stink in the compartment was penetrating because whoever had anything to smoke used some kind of inferior grade grown by the wayside. One could not openly smoke English or American cigarettes, as these had become the currency of the times. Safekeeping them like money was important if one possessed any.

It was immediately obvious that most people had not had any

access to a bath nor a change of clothes in some time. The war had robbed us of a lot: human dignity, pride, manners, and hope for survival to the next day, among other things. I felt like a dual personality. On one hand, I was a German girl having survived this terrible war, fully understanding and having lived through its demeaning tyranny. On the other hand, here I was with a native German—now a naturalized American—off to see the fields of heather where he was born and trying to see everything through his eyes, the Germany of his youth the way he must have remembered it. Now he would see it all shattered, torn, and divided.

He had packed an old suitcase full of hoarded rations from the PX: soap, shaving cream, shavers for the men, shoelaces, shampoo, cartons of cigarettes, two cans of tobacco for his uncle, cologne, chewing gum, chocolate bars, washcloths, towels, socks, nylons—you name it, it was in the suitcase. To secure it he had knotted a rope around it, not trusting the rusty lock. This chest was now resting on the shelf above his seat in the compartment and we kept a steady watch on it every time the train stopped at a major station. Too many shady characters were lurking about with the intent of spying. Intrigue was heavy in the air.

On the long train ride Bill told me about his earlier life in Oldenstadt. He said his memories of his life and home in Oldenstadt were limited because he was only eleven years old when he left for the United States. He confided that had his parents been more communicative on the subject, he would have been able to tell a much more vivid and interesting tale. Such as it was, he had to limit himself to bits of recalled conversation, local gossip, and, of course, personal experience. He said that in the US he could not remember his father recounting any stories or town gossip about the Old Country, much less personal memories. Then, too, he did not ask any direct questions about relatives or anything of that nature. He said that the people in the Lueneburger Heide, the region he hailed from, are as tight-lipped as you can imagine, especially toward strangers. On the other hand, they are honest, trustworthy, disciplined, frugal, and work harder than most people he knows. Their homes are neat and clean, and hospitality reigns.

From his diary Bill expounded further:

My great grandfather was born on a large farm in Moizen. I don't know how many children there were, but the oldest son always got the farm. My grandfather, the younger, received a sum of money and left to pursue the carpenter trade.

In his younger years he traveled a bit and, in what was known as the learn-and-wander years, made his apprenticeship and eventually became a master carpenter in Leipzig. After that, he settled in Oldenstadt and married Eliese Thiele in 1882. In the town register he was listed as a master carpenter. They had two children, my aunt Ella, born in 1885, and my father, born in 1888. The stone and brick house located in the center of town was on limited land, just enough to have a nice flower garden in the front. In the rear was an old barn. In 1917, the year before my birth, and the year before the end of World War I, children were considered a burden, another mouth to feed. My parents got married in 1916 while my father was still in uniform and he would only be home on short leave occasionally, until 1919. These war years, though, seemed to be the most colorful and exciting in his life.

To compensate for the lack of land, we rented about one-half acre at the edge of town. This supplied our need for most vegetables. In front of our house there were three wonderful apple trees, a half dozen gooseberry bushes, and flowerbeds. All of this was kept meticulously clean and neat. It was a matter of pride. In the far corner of the garden was a brick shed, dug out about three feet deep, where the year's supply of wood and coal were stored. Above it towered part of our neighbor's walnut tree. The house itself seemed spacious enough to accommodate both the grandparents and our family. They each had a separate entrance, with the carpenter shop in the middle as divider. My grandparents had a large kitchen with a rear door leading to the barn. Here about a dozen chickens laid their eggs in baskets that were nailed to the walls. Two pigs were kept every year in a stall right next to where the toilet was. I suppose this was quite an improvement compared to the former outhouse, but still we could see the rats skittering down below. Beside the kitchen was a comfortable living room with its lovely tile oven, and next to that was the bedroom. Many hours during the week were spent in the living room, where my grandfather played checkers or *Ziege*, a card game, with me. At dusk, when my grandmother no longer had enough light to darn socks and knit gloves, she would sing us lullabies until it was time for us to go to bed. One could walk through the carpenter shop without getting cold or wet. It was the route my brother and I took to the upstairs bedroom for the children. Though convenient, it was mighty cold up there during the winter months. I remember the last winter we spent there in 1928. It was so cold that our breath froze to ice on our down covers and the contents of the chamber pot under the bed turned to solid ice.

If either the bedroom or kitchen stove had been kept going during the night, it would have prevented us from shivering in bed. But it was considered too extravagant. Even though we already had electricity when I was born, it was not used. I believe it would have been too expensive, so we used our many beautiful kerosene lamps. My parents' section of the house consisted of three rooms, though most of their time was spent in the kitchen. There the center of attention was the cooking stove, which was actively engaged at all times. We children remember well the ritual of the Saturday night bath when the youngest went first, then my brother and lastly me. We were scrubbed clean all in the same bathwater but more warm water was added as needed.

Most of our furniture was made in the carpenter shop. Before my time, my grandfather had a helper working for him who also ate meals with the family and had his bedroom in the attic, where later my brother and I slept. Besides our small bedroom, the attic had many spacious and almost empty rooms. In the largest were kept two spinning wheels, a baby carriage, some carpenter wood supplies and other bric-a-brac. Another room held a steel helmet, swords, and uniforms from World War I. Two coffins were also ready at all times for my grandfather and grandmother. The coffins were sometimes sold as the occasion arose for others but always replaced again.

In those days it certainly seemed like a good and comfortable home to us. The whole property was enclosed in front with a white picket fence and in back was the barn. Between us and our neighbors, the Niemanns, was a brick wall, with about a yard of space in between for a corridor. In this corner of the property was the hand water pump conveniently close to the house. In the winter, even with all the straw around the pump, I still remember pouring hot water over it to defrost and prime the pump to get it going.

The carpenter shop separated the grandparents' apartment from ours. In the middle of the shop was a potbelly stove, where at all times a pot of glue was kept warm. All the boards were stored on sideboards above and occasionally a red squirrel would visit and hop between the boards. The tools were hanging on the side with all the varieties of wooden planes. In later years I used to keep a cage with two ravens on the tool bench, and those two were a delight to have. Wherever I went they would follow me. I found it amusing when they would pick at my grandfather's heel by the hole in his sock. That would get him hollering. I remember a photographer once coming to take some official pictures of me and my brother. What an ordeal that was. The man hid his head under a black cloth while we had to hold the pose until he squeezed the rubber ball in his hand. It seemed like an eternity went by.

In my grandparents' kitchen was also a large furnace-oven. Most of the time it was fired up for boiling the linens and washing clothes, except for several times in the winter when it was used for *Schlachtfest* (butchering) and cooking all the varieties of home-made wurst and sausage. This was always a lively time. After the pigs had been given a clean bill of health by the local vet, the butcher Burmeister came to the village. The animals usually weighed about 350 pounds. They were led out from the stall by a rope on one of their legs into the yard, placed on a seven-foot long wooden base, and stunned by a bolt to the forehead. The throat was cut and the blood collected for *Blutwurst* (bloodwurst). Lots of boiling water was used in tandem with a sort of bell-shaped instrument to get the bristles off the back. The pig was cut up and all the parts were brought to the kitchen. On a large table was mounted a hand-operated meat grinding machine. The butcher made all the cuts for the sausage, wurst, etc.

It used to be generally a two-day affair with everybody pitching in from morning till night. The first thing we tasted was the good soup. It was the broth in which the assorted wurst had been cooked. Sometimes a few of them burst and added flavor and substance to the broth. One had to make sure to stir the broth from the bottom up to get the hearty flavorful pieces. Several days later the *Suelze* (head cheese) was made, and some ham and sausages went to the smokehouse. These meat supplies had to last for the entire year until another couple of pigs had been raised for slaughter time.

During the rest of the year when the stove was used not only for cooking, but for washing clothes, the women prepared their homemade green soap just for laundry use. It took a lot of wood and briquets to keep the fire going. After the boiling of the wash, each item would be individually scrubbed clean, paying special attention to shirt collars, cuffs and handkerchiefs, then wrung out by hand and put into baskets onto a wheelbarrow. My mother would maneuver the load carefully down to the Wipperau River, which was about a fifteen-minute trek and not easy to balance. Luckily, the walk was all downhill. Upon arriving at the designated place by the river, the baskets filled with the wet linens were hauled onto a wooden platform extending into the stream, and there the clothes were rinsed in the cool water. When every item had been thoroughly rinsed and wrung fairly dry, it was again placed into the baskets. This time it was all uphill toward home.

When the weather was fair and sunny, some of the sheets and white items, like towels and other flat pieces, were spread on the lawn to bleach and hopefully dry. The rest was hung on the wash line to dry. Since most of it was made of linen, the wash line tended to sag in the middle from the weight. To prevent the linens from dragging on the ground, wooden poles were put up as supports under the clothes lines. The entire process seemed like quite a science but, naturally, depended heavily on cooperative weather. We children had to watch for any sign of rain approaching or, heaven forbid, the neighbor's geese or chickens marching across the linens on the lawn. Washdays were an all-day affair and slave work in comparison with today. Luckily such washdays took place but once a month and the rule of thumb was to have at least a dozen of everything clean on the shelf; one batch in use, another dozen in the dirty clothes hamper.

The Wipperau River flowing through our town and ending in Ilmenau could tell many a story. One summer, several of my father's friends played cards on one of those wooden platforms right in the middle of the river, with their feet dangling in the water. This was considered outrageously lazy and formerly unheard of.

The six oxen belonging to the local estate called Domaene were regular visitors by the water's edge to quench their thirst. These beasts of burden were of enormous size and mostly used for hauling rocks, loads of sugar beets, and similar work that required their notable size. Their loads were sometimes so heavy that their front legs almost lifted off the ground at the start of their pulling. Nevertheless, once underway they kept going their same slow and steady pace. By the time they eventually reached the river to drink, it would take a good fifteen minutes to fill their bellies. Once back at the barn and dining on some sugar beet *Schnitzel* (scraps), they would again be idly content.

During the ice-cold winter months, the older boys would try to play some tricks on the younger set, like daring them to put their tongue on the iron bridge railing. As a result, sometimes the tongue got stuck and the poor kids had trouble separating themselves from the railing. A bit of skin would tear away before this mischief ended. Today I feel so sorry about those shenanigans, but at the time it was one of the sporting things to do, I suppose.

My favorite pastime at the river was fishing. It only took a stick, a cork and a hook, along with a few yards of string, to have fun catching fish. The very best spot was in Meyerholz, near Domaene, where some wild turkeys occasionally laid their enormous spotted eggs. Standing there elevated a few yards above the river, with the sun shining through the beech and willow trees, one had a favorable vantage point to actually see the fish in the water.

After putting a little ball of sourdough bread on the hook I was ready for my prize! During the summer of 1927 I caught one of the largest trout ever angled at that spot. It made my grandfather so happy and proud to have such a whopper of a fish on his table.

On other occasions when the river had overflowed its banks, my father and I would go to spear the eels that remained on the meadow while the waters receded. Because they had not found their way back to the river yet, it was easy for us to catch them. Eels were always a delicacy, especially the jellied variety. Our favorite spot finding them was near the edge of the woods approaching Woltersburg. That was also the swimming area where in 1927 two teenage boys drowned. After cycling home from work and feeling hot and sweaty, they jumped into the water. One tried to save the other but both drowned. My father assisted in the search for the bodies, and they were later recovered.

In the winter, when the Wipperau was frozen, we enjoyed skating all along the river. The skates at that time were very simple and had to be clamped on to the shoes. No matter how one tried they never fit as snugly as desired. The key for tightening the skates was worn on a string around the neck, which was often a nuisance, and those keys were easily lost. To add more adventure, I would bring my large sled that my grandfather had made from a rocking chair. He put new runners of steel under that chair, and I had a wonderful sled. It was first used when beginning to skate in order to learn without the fear of falling. Eventually about half a dozen kids would hang on and sit on the sled to go up and down the river. While going under the bridge where the ice was a little thinner we would break through just a bit and get wet from the slush. Then it was a race to get home to the warm stove. Of course, we always got a lecture but in such a case a spanking was usually avoided.

Even the town's fire engine depended on the river. During the day the alarm was brought in by a fast bicycle rider; at night it was the night watchman, Tesken, who sounded the alarm with his cow horn. A team of horses galloped with the engine down to the river where the volunteers pushed one end of the hose into the water. It took two men at each end of the fire engine to pump and keep the pressure up. Hopefully the extension would be long enough to reach the fire.

In many incidents lightning was the cause of fires at barns and buildings at the edge of town. One time, lightning struck our neighbor's walnut tree. Hot nuts flew all around, exploding like firecrackers. The fire left a three-foot-wide burned-out track between the properties. When any wooden structure was burning it generally burned to the ground. During a fire the main thing was to keep it from spreading, so the damage to the building where it started was most severe. In those days houses had thatched roofs, which were ultimately declared unsafe. The fire insurance companies would no longer underwrite these structures. Roofs had to be tile or slate. After every fire the tavern was the meeting place, the source for news, gossip, and current events. All-day card games of *Skat* and plenty of rough talk made it the hangout for the fellows. The drinks and food costs were all written in the house ledger. The total bill for each of the carousers was customarily settled on the first day of the new year, to symbolize the start of the year without debt.

In our house we had a very large, cool, and serviceable cellar. The only entrance going down to it was from the grandparents' kitchen. In one corner of the cellar was a pile of some wood and coal. Another area held potatoes, turnips, and onions. A few five-gallon crocks contained sauerkraut and pickles. In another corner some apples and pears were stored. The varied combination of these stored items made for an altogether interesting aroma in the cellar. The bags of potatoes were donated by Onkel Heinrich, my mother's twin brother, who had a big farm in Woltersburg. All the rest of the produce came from our rented garden.

Our small village had only one grocery store. There we bought staples like sugar, *Malzkaffee* (malt coffee), and butter. If one had to go to the city of Uelzen, which was about five miles away, the bicycle was the usual mode of transportation. The farmers had their horse and wagon, but such an excursion was seldom considered. They bought their feed and hardware in large quantities in the city, as well as cloth. We had a seamstress come once a year for about two weeks, when she would make most of our clothing. Many people still had linen from past generations when flax was grown locally. Spinning and weaving had been a prosperous industry. Some of the finer linens had been made for the Royal House of England. We did not need to buy many new things because we either had them or made them ourselves.

School days were, for the most part, happy days. The school building was part of the church complex, which was built in 1857. It consisted of two rooms with large windows. One room was for children between the ages of six and ten and was headed by *Lehrer* (Teacher) Meyer. The other class was taught by *Lehrer* Mohwinkel for students aged ten to fourteen. Strict discipline was enforced by these two male teachers, who lived in apartments directly above the school rooms. The teachers knew not only their pupils thoroughly, but also their family situation and condition. Many children traveled for miles from neighboring villages that had no school facilities. During the cold winter months, it became quite an ordeal for the students; the warm potbelly stove in each schoolroom was a welcome refuge. On snowy days the stove would be surrounded by shoes of every variety to dry out for the later walk home. In the mornings, sometimes the teacher's wife kept a pot of hot chocolate milk on the stove to warm the children before classes began.

The basic toilet for the school was across the courtyard in a low, solid-brick building. Necessary newspaper (the toilet paper of the time) was supplied by the teacher's wife. On either side of the john was a goat and pig stall where some chickens had their residence, too. Across the street the teachers had been given a small plot of land for raising their own vegetables. The plot and their apartments were part of their salaries.

On Sundays during church services, *Lehrer* Mohwinkel took the collection and was responsible for the accounting of these funds. Once a week he directed and instructed the local glee club. Rehearsals were held in Steltzer's Tavern. My father was active in the group until he left for the United States. As a youngster he was a choirboy in church. After World War I and Germany's defeat he only went to church once or twice.

*Lehrer* Mohwinkel and my father respected each other greatly and were good friends. By age eleven my studies had included geometry, algebra, German history, the three Rs and some religious instruction. After I left Germany, I received no further instruction in the German language. We always spoke German with our parents and our dialect,

*Plattdeutsch*, was never forgotten.

Attending school wasn't all just sitting in the classroom. In the warmer months school hours were from 7 a.m. to 1 p.m. I think this was to give the boys and girls who lived on a farm the necessary time to help with the chores at home. During the winter months school started a little later in the morning and was let out about 3 p.m. Summer vacations were in July and August. The last year I was there I had the opportunity to work for Domaene and help with the care and cultivation of sugar beets. I was assigned to two long rows of the young plants and paid one mark per hour. I loved doing this work and was so proud to earn a few marks, but my Aunt Ella felt ashamed that a Schuette had to stoop so low and do work on the land for Domaene. On sunny days our school classes would sometimes take long hikes through the woods, where once we discovered a large *Huenengrab* (ancient Germanic burial site) among the hemlocks. We uncovered some of it but then stopped and reported this finding to the city museum. During our hikes some of us would pick mushrooms. We knew six edible varieties and they each were a delicacy.

In summer we always made time for the old swimming hole. My first swimming lessons I received from my father. I went into the water with his assistance while trying to go through the motions of swimming. All of a sudden, I noticed my father ten feet away from me and that was my first lesson. It took a while before I gained more confidence in that element. One summer I remember taking a class trip to *Bodensee* (Lake Constance). Our parents were quite willing to let us participate in such ventures. I had the feeling that they themselves would very much have liked to go, but there was the constant shortage of money.

The courtyard in front of the school was at one time a

church burial ground with about one hundred tombstones. During the 1920s only three or four large ones remained but now even they had been removed. We used this area for playing ball, running, and gymnastics. On one occasion I won the hundred-meter dash and was rewarded with a large heather wreath around my neck.

During the first few years in school, we used a slate board and chalk-like implement to write and draw. This could all be easily erased with a wet sponge. The trick was to preserve homework on the slate board and prevent smudging till it was returned to school and graded by the teacher. In later years we graduated to pencil, ink, and paper. The adjustment proved complicated. Dealing with ink blobs and making corrections was an annoying problem and one had to always carry blotting paper.

※ ※ ※

Suddenly the train slowed down. We had reached the border where American occupation ended and the British occupied zone started. Everyone had to get out at the next station. Luggage and passes were to be inspected. After all documents had been scrutinized and military regulations satisfied, we could board the train again. Bill asked me to talk now about my childhood, from the earliest period I could remember. It was going to be a long train ride ahead.

# CHAPTER 4

## *Still Aboard: My Childhood Reflections*

**I WAS BORN DECEMBER 29,** 1922, in an attic of a building where my maternal grandparents occupied a servant's apartment. It was located above an office adjacent to a factory that manufactured tools and related machinery. My mother had been in labor for forty-eight hours and attended on and off by a midwife who was also caring for another woman nearby in town. The midwife was the spouse of the local druggist, so she had more social influence and was given preferential treatment. Women preferred not to go to a hospital to give birth because too many died there of puerperal fever (commonly known as childbed fever).

When the labor dragged on and the midwife became concerned, she called a doctor to help matters along. There in that attic, my mother had a caesarean section with chloroform to put her out of pain for the duration. The doctor needed to ask my father and grandfather (who paid the doctor's fee) whose life to put first, the mother's or the child's. They decided the mother's life came first. In all the turmoil after the procedure, it is said that I rolled under the bed, and for a few moments I was *lost*. And as the tale went, my father refused to look at me for the first week because he had wanted a boy.

I did not know my father until the year I turned six. The situation was that my mother became pregnant and *had* to get married, consequently no church wedding could take place. The minister's study had to suffice for the marriage, and it was recorded on May 27, 1922. Many a stigma followed this event and bearing the brunt of it all was my mother. With World War I having ended four years previously, the following years saw a combination of inflation and recession; unemployment was at its worst. My parents could not find an apartment for almost six years after I was born. A person needed a permanent address to get a job and ironically could not get an apartment without proof of employment. So, my father lived at his parents' home and used their address and my mother lived with me in that tiny attic room above my grandparents' apartment, which only had room for the two of us. I felt great fondness for my maternal grandparents because they were the only family I knew as a young child. Their apartment and garden near the building were my world. Those years were spent with adult company. I became aware of children my age only when I was enrolled at the nearby Protestant kindergarten when I turned three, which was the age when kindergarten could start. What a revelation it was to see boys and girls my own age! None, however, had a brother or a sister; children were generally considered a burden, with times being so tough. Such a reality cast a shadow over every aspect of life. Children seemed so serious, and I felt we were born old. And we were all loners.

1937 Karola's maternal grandparents, Klara & Max Schroeder, 50th anniversary

My earliest recollection is being snug in bed in the morning while I watched my mother braiding her long hair, shaping it into a bun at the nape of her neck. I was very hungry and she warmed up a bottle of milk on the small potbelly stove in the room. She sweetened it with a bit of sugar and I couldn't wait to get to the bottom of the bottle, where the sugar taste concentrated. Another early memory is of being propped up in a baby carriage outdoors, looking up to the window where my grandmother waved to me with her smiling greeting. I will never forget how special it made me feel to have her lock me in her gaze and beam down her love, meant for me alone. What an event. To my recollection, I could not have been much more than a year old.

✳ ✳ ✳

Unexpectedly the train slowed to a halt. Our conversation quickly subsided. Fear of being overheard was acute and tension mounted. Nobody could be trusted.

It prompted me to think that here I was talking to a man

who had been a total stranger only weeks ago! I was going to an unknown destination, yet I could not help having the innermost sensation of feeling secure. During this quiet train interlude my thoughts wandered back to the event of my birth and how much it may have encumbered my mother. Was my existence the result of a true love affair? Was her original relationship with my father a one-time encounter, finding solace in one another during a sad and desperate era? Or was their union perhaps a means of finding understanding and caring by another human being, regardless of social status, financial means, and possible consequences? I would never know.

circa 1929 Karola's father        circa 1929 Karola's mother

Can the unborn child hear, sense, and absorb the feelings of the mother or events outside the womb? I believe so. As far back as I can remember I had an awareness of the senses. I always tried to be quiet, not be in the way, and not cause any trouble, just so someday I might be noticed and appreciated for just being me. But that never happened. The fact that my mother had to get married carried over into my life. Not for a moment was her lot forgotten by anyone around her. My mother was denied the thrill of being truly and openly courted, having a church wedding and the so-called proper sequence of these events. Under her circumstances this young mother-to-be had to sneak fresh air and outdoor walking exercise under the cover of evening darkness, just so neighbors would not prey on her with nasty gossip. She had not lived by the rules.

How could she handle all the old-fashioned baby-related laundry problems in that attic room for so many cold months yet ahead? I would never know. One did not ask grownups such questions, not even much later on.

As an infant I had an ear infection. I was not walking yet and my grandmother would carry me constantly. I remember clearly that she carried me to the kitchen window overlooking a linden tree and she sang so sweetly:

*Voeglein im Lindenbaum,*
*Singt leis', man hoert es kaum,*
*Singt doch so schoen . . .*

Translation:
Little bird in the linden tree,
Sings quietly, one hardly hears it,
But still sings so beautifully . . .

I forget the rest of the lyrics, but I can remember the melody if I try very hard.

This loving attention seemed the only soothing relief for the pain in my ear, probably along with some eardrops. It is amazing to me how clearly I remember some of these moments, despite being so young, so little.

I must have been such a quiet child. I cannot recall talking until I went to kindergarten, but I was constantly listening, and my mind never stopped absorbing and reasoning things out. What could a child say of any importance to a grownup? Children may only be seen, not heard, and most of the time not even seen.

Shyness was a great armor to wear, and quietness a shield to hide behind. Attending closely to spoken words, assimilating them, and attempting to arrive at their real meaning became my private game.

1928 Karola at age 5

1930 Karola (far rt.) at age 7

1934 Karola in neighborhood park

1937 Karola's confirmation at age 14

# CHAPTER 5

*Events Leading to Our Wedding*

**FROM OUR FIRST GET-TOGETHER ON** Christmas Eve in 1946, it took a long ten months and eight days until our wedding, though Bill had thought six months would be ample time to complete all the formalities. However, for a US citizen deployed as a military intelligence officer to marry someone from a country that was very recently an enemy was another hurdle. Everything had to go through Army channels.

We had become engaged on May 27, 1947, my parents' twenty-fifth wedding anniversary. By then I had met Bill's relatives in the British occupied zone of Germany. With his uncle, aunts, and cousins seemingly approving of me (as if Bill would have given them a choice!), and they doubtless having shared their opinions with his parents in Brooklyn, I felt like a piece of merchandise being inspected for a big sale. As this was Bill's first visit to his relatives after having left Germany as an eleven-year-old German boy, everyone now looked upon him as an American. Yet they were so surprised that he still spoke the native dialect *Plattdeutsch*. This was a definite plus in their eyes.

Bill wanted to show me as much of Germany as was possible under the travel restrictions that applied even to Allied personnel. Many times he smuggled me into the US mess halls just for a hot meal. He introduced me as a French visitor in civilian clothes, and to help I spoke a few sentences in passable French.

1947 Karola on bicycle outing

1947 Bill on bicycle outing

At the time of our engagement, Bill had to educate himself about all the possible (and impossible) heaps of paperwork necessary for him to get married to a conquered enemy. News had spread through the Allied grapevine of some marriages having been permitted, so there was hope.

The first official document, the letter of acquiescence, was filed April 12, 1947: *I wish to marry [name and address] because [insert reason]*. Each of us had to fill out the same form. What else would one have written other than *love* being the reason? Next came an interview for a character check with the senior chaplain of the headquarters command EUCOM, Major Carl F. Gunther. It took place at the IG-Farben Building in Frankfurt on April 15, 1947. In essence, Major Gunther recommended the approval of our marriage; further, he affirmed that a character check had been performed on me and it was not believed that this proposed marriage would bring discredit upon the military. Boy, they sure seemed to like me!

After that, Bill had to get character and conduct verifications on April 16 and, on the same date, file an additional form stating our intent to marry. It was yet another document to be piled upon the others already completed. With each signature certain rights and privileges for him were also lost. It was all designed to create a testing period for the couple, but mostly a test for him.

On May 5, 1947, the military government for Hesse, Liaison and Security Office Stadt und Landkreis, decreed that I had applied for a military exit permit at that office. It further stated that the CIC (Civilian Identity Certification) investigation of me had been forwarded with the application for the permit. As far as that office knew at the present time, I had been exonerated by the German Law for Liberation from National Socialism and Militarism. It was signed by Captain William J. Hammond, public safety officer. I had been exhaustingly scrutinized up until then. What next?

The same agency then issued an undated statement that they

had my military exit permit in their possession. It would be handed over to me upon their receiving written proof of the marriage.

Then came the intervals of painful waiting, with no news from any official either to Bill or to me. Finally, on October 16, 1947, we had to go for our medical tests at the headquarters medical dispensary in Frankfurt, which included blood tests and chest X-rays. After waiting for results again, we received a statement certifying that we were free from communicable disease.

For my next step, adding to the pile of forms already accumulated, I had to get my birth certificate. At the office of records in Offenbach I found they had, among other things, listed me as baptized a Catholic, instead of Protestant. Rectifying this longstanding mistake took more time and—of course—fees but eventually it was corrected.

During all the in-between waiting times we had given thought to how the wedding would take place. The minister who had confirmed me and knew our family well, Reverend Winkelmann, was consulted. The *Schlosskirche* (Castle Church) had been bombed into utter ruins. The only other church temporarily cleaned of rubble and offering a makeshift room usable for short ceremonies of baptisms, weddings, etc. was the *Friedenskirche* (Church of Peace).

Much earlier we had to think about our attire for the big day. Bill certainly was not going to wear his uniform, and I did not own anything appropriate, like a modest dress. Bill had the idea we would have matching tailored suits with white shirts, and that seemed the best possible solution. Possible—but only with everything from scratch at the nearest PX store. We went to a Heidelberg PX where suit material from England was available and purchased enough yardage, sewing thread to match, lining material, buttons, and zippers. Then Bill had to go over to the ladies' department of the PX (as everything was paid with allowable ration points by him) and get me shoes, nylons, and undergarments. How he managed this is still a wonder to me! It was a lot of back and forth in the PX that day, with many giggles by the salesgirls. I had to be invisible in a PX store because I was not yet a dependent of this American.

Way before our engagement, my parents, and most surely I myself, had begun to know how much Bill loved me and how deeply I had come to love him. Only in his presence was I truly happy. It seemed that I was coming out of an ice age. Feelings I had only dreamed about were really happening. This love also meant eventually leaving Germany. Yet this did not make me sad in the least. As long as I was with Bill, I felt truly assured that all would be well. This was in direct opposition to the gossips who, in their idle chatter, left not a shred of decency concerning any female consorting with an *Ami*, as the occupation troops were known (in our zone anyway).

❋ ❋ ❋

To get back to the story...

Eventually most people we came in contact with sensed there might be a wedding coming. Here was a major opportunity for them to procure cigarettes, the only currency for bartering on the black market. Slowly the offers came forward, including from my own family. The offer I found most hurtful was a used bridal dress, shoes and accessories, just to snatch those American cigarettes. Disgusting!

From this point forward people did not miss any opportunity to try to milk Bill (via me) for all kinds of goods, as well as offer favors, payable with the accepted currency and barter goods. They implied we would not be able to make do without their favors. Our biggest challenge now was where to find a reliable tailor in Offenbach to make our suits. We ultimately located the person through many a cigarette channel. When we heard his demand for cigarettes, butter, and coffee, Bill flinched. But this tailor had a good reputation and promised to do whatever he could. We had to go for many fittings, and each time he needed more goods to keep up his energy.

Finally, we had the suits in our possession! We had almost given up hope, but after such a layered process we were relieved about this ultimate accomplishment. It was one more thing that was finished and filled the time gaps of waiting for further document completion.

The wife of one of our neighbors had talked to my parents about what they planned to cook for our little wedding lunch at our apartment. Her husband would raise a rabbit for some meat on the humble menu, but he would need a carton of cigarettes, minimum. Well, Bill thought that would be nice, but asked him not to spread the news all over the neighborhood. The approximate time for maturing of the rabbit would be so and so long; now it needed food and supplies, which meant more cigarettes for Bill to get. When the big day of the attempted slaughter came, the rabbit allegedly bit the man on the arm. Medical attention was needed, plus more cigarettes for pain and suffering. We did have rabbit stew, however, for our wedding meal.

The same scenario seemed to be in the making for a bridal bouquet, from the planting of seed to the mature chrysanthemum! Who was smoking all of those cigs, anyhow?

Even though there was much yet to be planned, it was with a different kind of energy, with no more hopelessness in my life. The only fear remaining was that the Allied command might change their minds and not let us get married. But in spite of all this, we had to finalize the date in order to bring everything together. As soon as Bill's uncle up north in Woltersburg heard about the wedding, he was practically dictating to us who should be invited. When we told him there was only limited space in our bomb-shaken apartment and no extra food available, he still insisted they were coming with six people. Now it was Bill's headache where to house the entourage. One of the hotels in town, the Kaiserhof, had not been damaged too badly and was now occupied by the Allied forces. With all kinds of bribery Bill maneuvered a promise from one of the officers that space could be arranged for those relatives. As it turned out, they scored a whole floor. The understanding was that the usually boisterous bunch from the farm had to be super quiet, and especially *not speak German or get noticeably drunk* (if any alcohol should mysteriously get in their possession). Headache after headache! Only a few relatives of mine could attend the church ceremony, as the temporary space was too limited. The actual sanctuary, located upstairs, had also been destroyed. The entire church, therefore, was in shaky condition. The only parts still looking solid were the brass doors and the three church bells outside waiting to be hauled up at some future date to their tower again.

Bill's brother Johnny and his German girlfriend Heli would come up from Munich, where Johnny was stationed. An overnight stay was secured upstairs with Frau Besenbruch. Food for the whole group had to be coordinated. Bill kept a taxi from the CCD motor pool busy from morning to night—again for cigarettes and his ration points from the PX. To this day it is a wonder to me how Bill organized the entire enchilada!

These many to-dos kept us in such a tizzy, and they all revolved around everybody else. By the time the dawn of *our day* came, we were a bit exhausted. And yet, the to-dos seemingly were not over by a long shot. We needed about three taxis to chauffeur everyone to the church ahead of us. On that day, however, non-military taxis were scarce—only one was available. So, back and forth the taxi went, until it came to be our turn.

The civil ceremony had taken place earlier at the city hall (what was left of the building), from which we received the official marriage certificate. Now, we were back to the efforts of getting to the church on time. In those days, gasoline was not available for civilian vehicles, and every vehicle was converted to maximize fuel by stoking it with some bog-like material. This process produced a type of alcohol liquid by which the car could then run. The busy driver had to stop occasionally to repeat the stoking process. When we finally entered the readied taxi it went as far as rounding the corner one street removed from the church and came to a dead stop.

The only thing we could do at that point was to help the driver push the car a little further to the curb, put my white gloves back on, place my bouquet in my arm, and walk the rest of the way to the church. People were gawking, of course. The minister and everyone else in the church were wondering what had happened to us and were only too glad when we ultimately appeared. Reverend Winkelmann gave a most moving address before we said the final *ja*. A tenor sang a lovely solo, which was a surprise arranged for us by my mother's sister, Tante Greta. Many a sniffle could be heard from the congregation, and then it was all over. The relay transportation of those going to our apartment for lunch began anew, while we were whisked away to have our official photos taken, again for cigarettes and film.

Nov. 8, 1947 Karola and Bill's wedding

1947 Karola and Bill's wedding

By the time we returned to the apartment the minister had also arrived. Not to be a burden food-wise, his wife had declined our invitation. Reverend Winkelmann took home a sizeable package of sandwiches to make it up to her. The kitchen team was manned by Tante Greta, my cousin Willy Lutz, and Frau Besenbruch from upstairs. Willy was an accomplished cook and an apprentice baker who had the knack of making something out of almost nothing. Some of his baked masterpieces were prepared in advance at his home in Muehlheim, since we did not have a decent dependable stove. Everything at our place was makeshift. Bill played his accordion and a little dancing started up in our small entrance hall. How did we all do it? It had shaped up to be a nice little party after all. We then left the apartment and went to our honeymoon nest. Two of my girlfriends had offered to fix up the attic room at their apartment house, so that at least we had a place undisturbed and to ourselves. What a lovely gesture that was, although well paid for with cigarettes.

Our overnight honeymoon stay was in this cold and small attic room. Overhead the roof evidently had holes because on the floor were containers of different shapes and sizes to catch the rain, just in case. And rain it did. *Ping, ping, splash, ping*, in all rhythms with no stopping throughout the night into early dawn. But with a bottle of champagne all to ourselves, why would those conditions really matter?

The next day seemed like an ordinary day again. Bill wanted to travel with me to the now-separate country of Austria to give me a chance to say goodbye to my friend, Finki Bittermann, and her family. Also, he wanted to take me to the Bavarian municipality of Berchtesgaden for an actual Thanksgiving dinner in one of the occupied inns. Now that I was a relative of an American, I could penetrate these former walls of *No Admittance*, a new feeling of having gained a certain status, which was a good feeling and a wonderful reality.

Before we could prepare for this little trip, however, my Bill was obliged to settle the disturbances his relatives managed to cause at the Kaiserhof Hotel. It cast a shadow over what otherwise was a nice celebration for all of us. Unfortunately, he had to pay for their bad behavior and manners, not to mention the damages! It was lucky, indeed, that the whole mess did not end up in a military court. One cannot let bulls loose in a china shop, especially if those bulls do not speak English.

Diplomacy, diplomacy! Bill smoothed over the troubled waters with seemingly little effort. But I knew how upset he was about the people who had invited themselves, not given any thought about their behavior, but were still, after all, his relatives. The biggest blow was yet to come. They had left a wish list of what he should bring along next time he would visit them up north: two radios, many cartons of cigarettes, boxes of cigars, nylons, soap, coffee, pipe tobacco—you name it, it was on the list. As you can imagine, there was no follow-up visit after that. This was the last straw, the absolute finish. Hallelujah and Amen!

Instead, we packed two big suitcases with a lot of tradable goods for our visit to Austria, which for me was a final goodbye to my friends in Salzburg, this time as Frau Schuette. Finki Bittermann's parents did not think I should ever go such a huge distance, to America, from my parents or my home. What if I had to work very hard? They thought I would surely die of homesickness and certainly I was not prepared to be a *Hausfrau und Mutter* (housewife and mother), in their minds, anyway. What if? What if?

No one except Bill knew I was to become a mother by July or so of 1948. With all those mixed opinions around us, we thought it wise to keep this precious secret to ourselves. With Bill's departure to the States just around the corner, we had enough things to handle. He had to leave before me, but not until he was certain those hard-to-come-by travel papers were confirmed and in my possession, and my trip as his wife was assured.

# CHAPTER 6

*First Turkey Dinner*

**I HAD NO INKLING THAT** one could actually eat turkey or that they were raised for human consumption. After the war, when I was employed at the CCD (Civil Censorship Division) as translator between the American occupation forces and the German employees, my ignorance was corrected. The mess hall was in the basement of the building. The first floor held the offices where the incoming and outgoing mail was scrutinized. Of course, the censor business had to be done by Germans and they were, for the most part, hungry if not outright starving after many years of food rationed to the point of basically nothing.

After people began regularly fainting when the preparation of food wafted fantastic aromas upstairs, the management allowed one warm meal served for a small fee to the German personnel on a daily basis.

But coming back to those turkeys . . .

Beginning in November 1945 there was a lot of delivery activity, all headed to the kitchen downstairs. These massive deliveries were to be for what they called Thanksgiving and the star of this festive meal was the turkey. We *Krauts* were dumbstruck about all this since none of us were familiar with the holiday. We were only given the day off and that meant no warm noonday meal.

Fast forward to November 1947. Unbelievably, I was by then married to one of those occupation fellows. A short honeymoon trip of three days to Salzburg, Berchtesgaden, and Munich followed a week later. At Haus Geiger in Berchtesgaden I was to experience my first American Thanksgiving feast. The hotel was operated by Austrians strictly for Americans and other authorized persons like me. I can only describe this fairytale event as opulent after coming out of years of what one could only describe as subhuman existence.

The meal, the presentation of same, the service, the view of the majestic mountains covered with the mantle of glittering snow—ah, can I take it all in! The atmosphere was a cautious and quiet one because there might be a spy in disguise nearby trying to overhear any coded conversations. The awe of savoring this luscious cuisine, some of which I had never seen before, was definitely overwhelming. Though I did not want to miss any course offered, I had enough sense not to overeat. How was my stomach going to handle it? This was my first acquaintance with turkey and all the trimmings.

Bill and I took a robust walk afterwards. It was cold outside, and the snow under our boots crunched with every step. An insistent brisk wind soon compelled us to head back. Haus Geiger was warm and oh so comfortable! Just before we reached the hotel, we met a chimney sweep. What a good luck sign for us! In Germany, chimney sweeps are considered good luck—as are pigs and ladybugs. We took his picture and he didn't mind posing for a pack of American cigarettes.

✳ ✳ ✳

Soon would come the time to depart for America, but not the two of us together. Bill was required to leave ahead of me on a different troop transport, *The Holbrook*. I would first have to go to Bremerhaven and be quarantined with other war brides for a few days. Then, I would embark on a troop transport to the land of freedom.

After Bill left for the States, I was preparing for my train trip to Bremerhaven, where all war brides went through three days of quarantine, vaccinations, examinations, final ration points for the PX (I was now eligible, oh boy), more papers, and generally killing time before boarding the troop transport, the *General RE Callan*. We were about forty or so war brides among the GIs on board and we had the privilege of special quarters.

On December 18, 1947, I waved goodbye to the country Hitler had brought to devastation. Would it ever be rebuilt? Maybe in a hundred years or so, or never. It looked so totally hopeless.

The future lay ahead for me with my dear Bill. It was strange how easy leaving my home was.

# CHAPTER 7

## *In Transition*

**DURING MY DAYS OF QUARANTINE** in Bremerhaven I observed quite a few different types of war brides. I shared sleeping quarters with one who had a baby. For the three nights of our stay, I could not get much sleep. When the baby finally dozed off the mother would promptly start crying, so overcome was she with homesickness. Why wasn't I crying or sad, she wanted to know. Hmm. It was not worth talking about. She seemed like a person incapable of understanding anyone else's condition. And then, the smell of soiled diapers almost did get me to cry.

During the day I was busy with scheduled activities and things to do, as well as getting promptly to meals (we even had a choice of menus). I used my privilege of purchasing cigarettes and other precious items, made a package for the folks at home, sent it off, and dreamed of what they could do with these goodies. Months later I found out they never received the package. It probably never left the post office, which was a big disappointment for me.

Before leaving Offenbach, my final duty was to present myself at the police department to receive clearance papers confirming I had no police record. Amazingly, these files must have been kept more secure and safe than human beings. The officer in charge made a major point of informing me that if I were sent back from Bremerhaven, or was refused entrance to America, my eligibility for food stamps and other rations would be nil. He had to rub it in that now I was considered a stateless person and no longer had any rights. Wow, did he hate those war brides, those whores. At that moment I realized, no matter what happened to me in America, I would never come back. I would make a life somehow. I wanted to finally be stepping into freedom, the future with my Bill, regardless of eventual hardships!

The dawning of day four arrived; time to get packed to board the ship. With military precision we were the last allowed to go aboard, all of us stateless traitors, leaving, leaving. The GIs threw packages of cigarettes into the water. A few hardy Germans dove into the cold brine after them, clothes and all.

Such a display demonstrated how great the need was in Germany for basic survival and the means to obtain it. It was a little too sadistic to be funny, but the GIs were so happy to be on their way home! And they had certainly learned the value of cigarettes during their tour of duty. For many families they had been lifesavers and continued to be for a long time to come.

The military band played:

*Muss i denn, muss i denn*
*Zum Städtele hinaus, Städtele hinaus*
*Und du mein Schatz bleibst hier!*

Translation:
I must, I must
leave the city, leave the city
while you, my darling, remain here!

As I stood in line to board the transport vessel, the feeling of history—my own personal history—was profoundly present, but the well-known tear-jerking farewell songs somehow did not touch me. This was a moment I would never have dreamed of, a moment many German girls had even calculatingly attempted to maneuver. But now the dream was actually happening to *me*! All in the time span of not quite a year.

What was I leaving behind? Oh, so many memories; people who had shaped my life, many now dead. But I did not leave things behind. Material things had either been lost or totally destroyed. How quickly possessions had become unimportant while bombs hailed relentlessly from above. Now, however, with the cessation of war the acquisitions gained greater value if they amounted to more than those of your neighbor, so the fear that made us all equal during the bombing raids was now over and forgotten. Greed, lying, stealing, and keeping the acquired goods a secret were all commonplace.

A feeling of guilt was also present. Who had to clean up the destruction, not to mention do the rebuilding? They were the ones deserving medals and special respect. And they had to labor in a constant state of hunger. Who would ever honor the innocent women and children, as well as the men killed on the home front? They were all forgotten heroes.

My luggage consisted of a small travel bag and a slightly bigger suitcase containing some necessities, two crystal wine glasses (one red, one green) that Bill had bartered at the cigarette market with coupons, and a ceramic candleholder (a little Black boy holding a candle), all carefully wrapped in undergarments. The other invisible luggage I carried safely inside me—our child who would be an American citizen at birth. This was my most important carry-on.

To what was I traveling? To my unknown future, my life with Bill, having a family; to freedom, the freedom to fail or succeed;

to happiness, peace, contentment, no bad moods, no anger, no dictatorship. How would people receive me? Would they still see me as the enemy, perhaps a Nazi, or just not accept me, period? Every country has its own propaganda. I definitely was aware of possible rejection. Yet with Bill by my side, and having the best of intentions, I felt it would all work out. One of Bill's favorite sayings was, "Everything happens for the best." He was always so supportive. I could feel his energy coming to me from Brooklyn, where he had arrived before me. My mind's eye saw him waiting there for me, his love drawing me toward him and my new life.

Reverend Winkelmann had quoted from the Book of Ruth at our wedding:

> For whither thou goest, I will go . . . thy
> people shall be my people, and thy God
> my God; where thou diest, will I die, and
> there will I be buried; the Lord do so to
> me and more also, if ought but death
> part thee and me.

While still waiting in line for processing there was no conversing among the war brides. One day earlier we had been examined again, which verified my pregnancy and the fact that I had not picked up any illness. Smallpox vaccinations were also administered. We were fingerprinted, followed by more questionnaires to be filled out; there was continual mistrust, standing in line for our turn, and waiting for the next girl. The tedious process could become very depressing at times, but I did not let it get to me. I kept my great destination in mind.

While entering one door and exiting the other I saw a familiar face, Ingeborg Seifert, now Simpson, a friend from Offenbach! She was so happy to see me. She had gone to see my parents to say goodbye to me but found out I had already left for Bremerhaven.

She had married Paul Simpson, who worked as an Allied civilian in CCD. *Now we were both bound for America!*

We were hoping to be on the same troop transport, but according to her scheduled arrival time she had two more quarantine days. We exchanged our American addresses and promised each other if and when we were homesick or bored (ha, no chance!), we would write to each other. Two war brides bound for The New World. I did not tell Inge about my pregnancy for fear she might want to gossip in a letter home. It was our secret, mine and Bill's.

Two vessels were docked in the harbor for transporting GIs and stateless persons. I had hoped the larger one would be the one for me, but no such luck. Earlier the captain had addressed war brides separately about the length of the voyage, the route, and the foreseeable weather conditions. He would take the southern route (whatever that meant, but it sounded good). The crossing would take approximately eight to ten days (oh my God, *that* long?). The captain described our quarters with apologies. It was, after all, a troop transport. Don't expect any luxuries.

Finally, the line started moving. Schuette, Karola . . . next! Present your visa! Please board now! So, there I went, following orders and directions to my assigned sleeping quarters (with three other gals in the smallest room): two bunk beds, a small sink, a metal mirror above it, and four small lockers. That was the space to be shared for the trip. Since I was pregnant, a lower berth was assigned to me.

Much militaristic shouting of orders finally guided the other three girls in, and we began to settle into the meager space. After exchanging first names and noting the location of the *head* (a new word I learned for "toilet on a ship"), time had gone by and, aha, the ship was moving. The small room had become quite stuffy and one of the girls was feeling ill. Oh no, she was seasick, a very contagious malady!

The southern route, the captain mentioned, sounded like calm waters ahead, but one of the guards on the vessel had talked about eventually circumnavigating stray mines, etc. This aside was not meant to be overheard and I was sorry my hearing was so acute.

What did erase worry about these things very quickly was . . . uh-oh, *mal de mer* (sea sickness) . . . I had made my mind up that I would not let it affect me, and we had not even passed the White Cliffs of Dover when it struck! All the thinking I had planned to do on this long trip was no longer possible. I could not even get my thoughts to function—no dreaming about the moment of meeting Bill on those far away shores. Just get to the head and maybe stay there. By God, it was so bad I thought I was going to give birth by mouth. Somehow the ship's nurse placed me in sickbay. I didn't see daylight or the deck for the rest of the trip.

After all the administering of tests, my vaccination site had become slightly inflamed. The sea had become violent after I don't know how many days and nights. Even holding onto the sides of the narrow bunk could not prevent rolling and bumping against what I thought had become my casket without a lid. No nurse showed up to pamper us or offer any food. Their policy was that unless you get up, get dressed, and get to the officers' mess hall, no food will be brought to you. Our sea sickness was just in our minds. These were real battleaxes. Surrounded by the battleship's depressing gray interior, one could not help but feel deserted. Abandoned to the misery, just hoping to survive it, a comatose condition set in, interrupted only by the horrible heaving.

How vast a distance must I have come? Will I ever get there? Alive? If I ever get to New York, I might not be strong enough to walk. I would so like to kiss the ground and then die in peace, just knowing I had made it to the land of freedom and into the arms of *my love*. It was still oh so far away. I knew I had lost a lot of weight, judging by how weak I felt, or was it the constant rolling of the ship making me so unsteady?

My few belongings and toilet articles were back in the suitcase, stashed in the locker of my assigned cabin. If I had been able to get to the shoddy mirror nearby, I probably would not have recognized myself. Since there was no possibility or even wish to do anything, just surviving the next moment had become my only priority.

Occasionally I fell into short, fitful, delirious moments of sleeping, or was it fainting? But these intervals passed quickly, changing from hallucinations back to reality. Actual measurement of time had been lost back on the shore at Bremerhaven. Should I survive this trip, I vowed to never set foot on a ship ever again!

＊ ＊ ＊

The turmoil of the ocean and the fury of the gales were a sheer hell to endure. The ship's propeller was more than once out of the water and one expected certain doom any moment. There was no reassuring sense we would recover from any of this. To make matters worse, my smallpox vaccination got badly inflamed because of the violent motion, even in my sick bay bunk. A few of the girls suffered miscarriages during this trip because of the violent motion of the ship. It was getting near Christmas Eve day, not that it made any difference, but by now we must have been about mid-ocean. On Christmas Eve one of the GIs from the mess hall stuck his head in and threw a couple of packs of cigarettes on our beds with a hearty "Merry Christmas." It was such a welcome gesture, as human contact seemed very rare, and the guy had taken a chance. Any contact with us by them was off limits. I looked at the cigarettes, thinking what they would buy for my parents back home—at least the next week's meals! I wasn't even a smoker and if I were, I was too sick to care for a puff.

Suddenly, the door opened, and I received a ship-to-shore radiogram (actually, it was shore-to-ship) with a message from my dear Bill wishing me Merry Christmas and he would meet me upon arrival. This message was my lifeline for the rest of the trip. I clung to it with all my heart and soul.

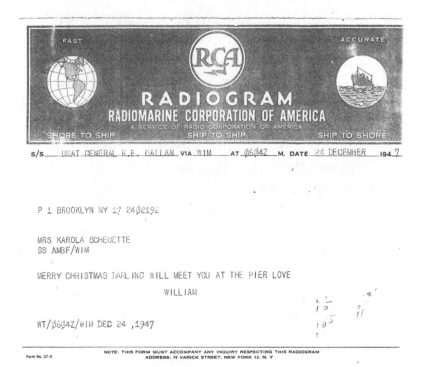

FAST                                            ACCURATE

**RCA**

**RADIOGRAM**

**RADIOMARINE CORPORATION OF AMERICA**

A SERVICE OF RADIO CORPORATION OF AMERICA

SHORE TO SHIP           SHIP TO SHIP           SHIP TO SHORE

s/s___ USAT GENERAL R.E. CALLAN VIA WIM ___ AT 0604Z ___M. DATE 24 DECEMBER ___ 194 7

P 1 BROOKLYN NY 17 2402192

MRS KAROLA SCHEUETTE
SS AMBF/WIM

MERRY CHRISTMAS DARLING WILL MEET YOU AT THE PIER LOVE

WILLIAM

WT/0604Z/WIM DEC 24 ,1947

Form No. ST-2    NOTE: THIS FORM MUST ACCOMPANY ANY INQUIRY RESPECTING THIS RADIOGRAM
ADDRESS: 75 VARICK STREET, NEW YORK 13, N. Y

1947 Christmas Eve radiogram from Bill to Karola

I was thinking of my parents and some of my other relatives back home. It was a good thing they could not see me like this. I was praying not to lose the baby that I was carrying, knowing the fate of some of these girls, and the trip was not over yet. There was merrymaking aboard the ship. The singing became quite loud and I assumed that some of the fellows had smuggled liquor on board. They were certainly crafty about that. Since this was a troop transport, liquor was taboo for fear of fights and resulting issues. It turned out that one of the soldiers thought he was finding additional libation by drinking from a bottle labeled as aftershave lotion. He was so sure it was just a camouflage, but it was the real stuff. He died that very evening. His casket was put right next to us in sick bay where a swinging door separated it from the head. The casket was chained to the wall so it would not slide all over creation, or possibly into the slushy mess that was ever present on the floor; the plumbing had failed as soon as we hit open sea.

In the early mornings we were visited by a really nasty, tough nurse telling us that this business of sea sickness was only in our heads. She gained great delight out of saying that if we wanted to eat we would have to get our behinds to the officers' mess hall, but we could not even stand any smell of food, anyway. In reality her kind was just so resentful that we, the former enemy, had managed to acquire a husband, while she was still ignored.

One of the guys on kitchen duty began to feel quite sorry for us and made it his business to inform the ship's doctor of our plight. By now I had lost at least twenty pounds and looked awful. This was December 27, and there was a general commotion to put the entire vessel in shipshape condition. We were the only ones that looked too hopeless to be shipshape, but this nice fellow's concern was more evident than most others would express. He was telling us that if we could not leave the ship on our own two feet, we would be quarantined on Ellis Island. That was known back home as Devil's Island or the Island of Tears. He did not back down until he knew the doctor had seen us. The doctor was appalled that he had not been informed of our situation. He was very kind and spoke with us reassuringly and prescribed a sleeping pill for me so I could get a good night's sleep. It would have gone on his record if we had been neglected any further; this was already bad enough. We could tell he was also concerned about that casket near us. I did not envy him the reports he had to fill out.

※ ※ ※

We were to arrive the next day in America. I was so weak, barely able to get off the bunk to stand on my two legs, and I knew that I had to pack my humble suitcase and travel bag. The ship was still rolling but not quite as bad as the past nine days. Some other friendly soul finally packed those items for me because the only thing I could manage was to crawl on all fours. Then there were procedures to attend to, like hearing in what order to leave the ship upon arrival. Also, there was what they called a head tax to be paid in the amount of fifty dollars and I had no money! I feared I was a candidate for immediate deportation. The ship's crew took in all this pandemonium with amusement but they managed to have a serious look on their faces. My hopes to see my Bill fell to the bottom of the ocean. I could not hold back my tears and soon they were spilling out from this dehydrated shell-like mortal. Miraculously, there was a representative of the American Red Cross aboard who told me they would lend me the money and I would be duly admitted to America. They stamped my Military Dependents Visa with the word *ADMITTED*. I was to be let into the land of milk and honey, and the land of unbounded possibilities.

After a ten-day trip from Bremerhaven, Germany, and an exceptionally stormy crossing (the captain later confessed), my hopes as a *stateless* person and *war bride* began to perk up. I might actually make it to shore, kiss the ground, and then die.

# CHAPTER 8

*My Arrival in America: December 28, 1947*

**THE MEDICATION HAD SERVED ITS** purpose. Even though it was a drugged sleep, it made me able to go through the duties and demands that this important event required. I had to get back to my assigned cabin, get my things together, and—most importantly—get myself dressed. Every few minutes I had to sit down, feeling so exhausted by the slightest effort. I did not dare look into a mirror. If I really made it to solid ground and could stand to face Bill, would he recognize me? And then I had to meet his family, if I actually got that far. I was scared. Waiting in line to go ashore was endless because war brides were the last to get off. First, all officers and US citizens, then GIs, Allied personnel, then we hapless greenhorns were allowed to proceed.

Earlier we had been informed that the entire New York area had been hit by the worst snowstorm of the decade, which explained our rough time at sea. When we could spot the coastline, everything looked covered with a white blanket, including the Ferris wheel and the parachute jump at Coney Island, which I had heard about. My most overwhelming impression was steaming by the Statue of Liberty. I was crying. Mere words could not describe my emotions. She unflinchingly and majestically welcomed me, this bundle of misery that came from the country Hitler had just trashed. I wanted to be so worthy of that welcome.

I don't know who carried what, if it was my suitcase and travel bag holding me up or if it was my heavy old plush coat giving me shape and my hiking boots supporting me. I actually made it down the endless gangplank. I would have made it somehow, even if I had to crawl on all fours. It was freezing cold and slippery underfoot. I tried to find somebody in the distance resembling my dear love, Bill. Suddenly, somebody took my humble luggage and lifted me up in a huge embrace. I was home!

My poor sweetheart must have been waiting for hours in the bitter cold and he looked blue in the face. We surely were a sight. Since it was a Sunday and just a day after the bad snowstorm, there was not a single vehicle in view, except an old army bus. The driver took pity on us and gave us a lift to the next running subway. I was completely drained and worn out. With every step I was functioning like a robot but thinking like a desperate human: *Where is that subway?* Finally, we were able to locate a train, and by God, here I was swaying and tossing again like on the boat, and overhead were all those ads for food. I also felt disgrace hanging over me! For certain everybody must see that I had just arrived from Hitler's Germany. I felt so guilty for everything he had done to the country of my birth. We had to change trains and the agony of sea sickness kept me concentrating on not throwing up in the train. The growing realization that I was finally in the United States made me wish I felt my very best in this moment, so that my health and well-being would be on a par with this monumental occasion. And ahead I still had to meet my in-laws!

After what seemed an eternity, Stewart Street in Brooklyn was near. Snow drifts had undone the attempt to clear the streets. As a result, the trek from the last subway exit to the apartment house was like a cross-country ski hike. Bill and I did not engage in much conversation during our efforts, since each of us was struggling to keep from falling and I was plainly too fatigued.

With all that occurred we had never really discussed the apartment his parents occupied, nor the neighborhood there. I had not formed a picture in my mind as to how it might be. My idea was to keep an open mind and make the best of any given situation. After all, staying with his parents was only temporary until Bill could find something suitable in the way of a job. His mother had written such a wonderful and touching letter of invitation to us in Germany so I thought that everything would be manageable. I remembered, though, to ask him if he had told his parents that I was expecting. He said he had wanted to wait until I was finally here and keep our sweet secret a little while longer. That was fine with me. I did not show yet anyway.

Huffing and puffing, I climbed three flights of stairs, trying not to let the dim and poorly maintained landings depress me. Bill opened the door and there we were. I found myself in the eat-in-kitchen. His parents welcomed me very cordially, yet my intuition told me they would not care for an embrace, just like where I came from. It had taken my departure to America to get farewell embraces and emotional hugs from my parents. They had a hard time showing emotion. They were brought up to believe this was a gaudy display and an admission of weakness. I guess I presented a pathetic sight: weak from weight loss, dehydrated, and undernourished, still reeling with sea legs, and unclean from no bathing during the whole ordeal. Adding to that the infected sinuses and an inflamed vaccinated arm, what could one think of such a heap of humanity? And there was no second chance for a first impression. My only aim at this point was simply to sit down, go into limbo, or better yet, crawl into the nearest hole.

I was shown to the living room. At first, I thought this was just the end of the hall, but it was the living room, the end of the apartment. It was called a railroad flat. As soon as I could sit down—though it must have been more of a collapse—everything went hazy. Right then, my newly met mother-in-law wanted to dish up a hearty meal. I could not rouse myself to their urgent invitations to eat with gusto (the smell of food making me ill again), which disappointed my in-laws deeply. Sensing this, of course, I started to cry and once started I could not stop. Their thoughts seemed to permeate the air: what kind of a sick weakling had their son imported from the Old Country? Would they be stuck with this for a while?

So many thoughts swirled in my head. *How will I get my strength back? How and when will I be able to write home about my arrival? How can I honestly describe it?* To compose a happy letter I had to force my thoughts to be still. The next day would be my twenty-fifth birthday—*God give me strength!*

Dec. 29, 1947 Brooklyn, Bill and Karola on her 25th birthday,
one day after arriving in America

The living room still bore evidence of the Christmas that had just passed. The tree and some empty gift boxes were there but the feeling of Christmas had gone out of the place, if it was there to begin with. This was to be our bedroom for a while. A three-quarter bed was positioned in the corner near the door that connected to the small bedroom behind it, which was my mother-in-law's. Her bed was headboard to headboard with ours. There was just a thin wall in between. The connecting door did not close properly. In addition, the door had to be kept open to let the remaining heat from the kitchen stove through, since there was no central heating, and the kitchen was at the opposite end from the living room. My father-in-law's tiny bedroom was between his wife's bedroom and the kitchen, with the bathroom next to the kitchen. Making a trip to the bathroom at night meant parading past everybody else's bed. These conditions did nothing for intimacy, not to mention even whispering sweet nothings.

Before spending my first night in America I had to have a bath. This caused considerable inconvenience, like firing up the boiler over the kitchen stove so the hot water could reach the ice-cold bathtub, and providing towels and soap. I could only go through this procedure with Bill's help, as I was too weak to function and had to be careful of my infected vaccination. Shampooing also had to be performed in the tub. The few clothes in my suitcase had all taken on the body odor of my one and only nightgown worn throughout the crossing. Consequently, I had to borrow a nightgown. Mine, which had originally been sent to me in a care package along with other items, had previously arrived with other distinctive aromas (salami, ham, coffee, etc.) and had attracted little critters wanting to share in my goodies. They chewed a hole into the nightgown at the most awkward spot imaginable. Yes, right *down there*. Another wonderful first impression! Well, I could not worry about that. I felt clean after such a long time and now I could go to bed and hopefully have a peaceful sleep. There was not much room in this small bed; we had to turn around at the same time and stay in the same spot. I was in America, in the arms of my love, and I felt at home as long as he was there. I did not miss anything. This was my safe haven, no matter the circumstances.

I must have slipped in and out of sleep with dreams and a nightmare that I was still on the ship. The ship could not dock anywhere, it was rolling, and there was a distinct feeling of seasickness about to strike again. I woke early; the room was so cold, and I asked Bill if I had imagined that the room was shaking. He said no, the subway goes right underground, under Stewart Street. It was now Monday morning and Bill said he would have to leave and would be back a couple of hours later. He would not explain why, so I was left alone with my mother-in-law. His father had already left for work earlier. I simply did not know what to do, say, or, for that matter, how to act. I tried to close my eyes and think about all the happenings during the last weeks. Sleep now eluded me because of the overpowering events that had taken place. They had happened to *me*, the little nothing from bombed-out Offenbach, the wallflower nobody looked at twice.

The ice-cold room brought me to my very present reality: I was freezing, pregnant—yet alone—missing Bill, and twenty-five years old. *Happy Birthday to me!*

I heard Bill come back. He presented me with a beautiful gold ring, set with a single pearl, and a Happy Birthday kiss. Then he made me breakfast, starting with a grapefruit, followed with toast, jam, and coffee. Only then did I realize how long it was since I had eaten. My stomach was feeling quite surprised and, after so long a fast, I could manage only very little food. I then overheard that my sister-in-law was coming to meet me. She was staying nearby with a former girlfriend, for lack of room at home. I was to be looked over by her, as if I were on exhibit, and I knew by intuition I would be at a disadvantage. Again, borrowed clothes would have to do because my meager wardrobe had to be sent to the cleaners. All these conditions did not lift my spirits. I felt I was the low man on the totem pole but had to make the best of it.

I could not help feeling like an intruder involved in some kind of competition to gain favor with the management. On top of the constant indoor stress, the weather outside provided mostly snow and sleet as the prevailing forecast. I felt trapped by circumstances within a most critical environment. The confinement was hard to take. The lack of privacy was the toughest, along with no funds of my own. I had never before experienced dependency to such a degree and it was not conducive to making me at ease or open to good conversation.

While Bill was gone earlier my mother-in-law tried to draw me out about my former job, my financial situation, and so forth. She could not comprehend the conditions in Germany after the war and why the good old Deutsche Mark could not be brought to this country and exchanged for dollars. The parents had hoped Bill would marry a rich farmer's daughter, so eventually they could all go over there again. That I was a city girl did nothing to elevate my status, since one cannot trust the morals of city girls! But then again, she mentioned that Bill probably had many girlfriends in America. There was a definite attempt to alienate me right in the beginning, since I seemed (and rightfully so) nothing but a huge liability. Then the whole litany surfaced as to how tough their beginning was in this country when they first came over in 1929, just so I would not have any inflated ideas about being in America. What did my father do for a living? How did my parents feel about my going away? The grilling was not out of compassion but out of jealousy, distrust, and fear of losing a former provider for the family. As an only child reared under a very strict regimen, my lines of defense were not well developed. But suddenly I discovered that I possessed a certain resilience. I did not fall into all these traps of intimidation. I was not married to my in-laws, even though I respected them for creating my Bill. As long as he stood by me, the whole world could take me on, and I it.

The phone rang: it was the Red Cross. A friendly voice

instructed me to strictly answer with a yes or no. Their concern was how I had found my situation so far, if it was satisfactory and if everyone was nice and good to me. On their records it also showed that I was expecting a baby and they would waive the fifty dollar head tax if I was willing to enroll in a Red Cross course for infant and baby care. I made the proper enrollment appointment for the nearest date when the streets were passable. Then these total strangers wished me a Happy Birthday.

In the coming days I tried to make myself useful, offering to help with washing, cooking, and cleaning, but was firmly declined. It made me feel most incompetent and useless. I could not wait for the weather to improve to get out of this prison-like environment and to be able to have a private conversation with my husband. There were so many questions in my mind about everything and everybody. Most of all I could not understand the cold behavior of my mother-in-law, comparing it with her former kind invitation to be a guest in their apartment until we could be on our own. Bill, too, was seeing his parents from a totally new perspective. He had a hard time coming to grips with this realization.

Every Monday Bill disappeared for a few hours in the morning, which I found most mysterious. The explanation for this was that he picked up his unemployment money at the so-called 52/20 Club. It meant $20 for 52 weeks. I felt so bad that he had gotten me this ring for my birthday, especially because the financial status of his family seemed so wanting. He said he gave the unemployment money to his mother for groceries, and the ring he had afforded by shoveling snow.

The agony of not being able to contribute to the family until Bill would have a job and we would be out of the house was constant. To make matters worse, I hated to ask Bill for any kind of pocket money, but I had not a dime to my name. I had held a job ever since my fourteenth year, always saving most of my income, contributing to my parents' household funds and just keeping a little pocket money for myself. Not having any money now made me feel like a beggar.

Then came the day when we told his parents that we were expecting a baby. It was like the roof had fallen in! They felt too young to be grandparents and we better get going and move out; there was no room in the inn. We had to disappear when their card-playing friends came for weekly afternoon sessions so I would not cause all kinds of unwanted questions by their peers. Did Bill have a job yet? On these days I walked the streets of New York, not really sightseeing but being heartsick. I had to contemplate all the possible outcomes in this family matter. The one time I let my in-laws know how I felt was when the home atmosphere became particularly icy. I told them that if I had known their true feelings toward their daughter-in-law, I would have never set foot in their place.

In reality they were probably just upset that there was nothing to brag about to their friends. However, it was their friends who almost forced my in-laws to introduce me to them, and that in turn made them feel ashamed they had hidden me for so long. Suddenly, the climate on the home front became friendlier. I was allowed to help with household chores. The biggest hit I finally made was through my knowledge of knitting. My mother-in-law had started a sweater for her better half but could not follow the instructions in English. Within a snowbound week the sweater was completed. My elevated status in their estimation was just short of a miracle!

Another saving grace was the courses at the Red Cross. There I found out what fate some of the other war brides had encountered. Some were shipped back, the reason being that their fiancés were Black. In those days no marriage was allowed between Whites and Blacks. It was the law. Some who had traveled on to the Midwest found that they were lured to this country into such poverty that they could not stand it. In these cases the Red Cross provided the funds and assistance for return transport to Europe and their families. Comparing my lot to these unfortunate souls, I came off exceedingly well! Regardless of what happened to me, I would have *never* gone back. This was now *my* country.

These caring people at the Red Cross arranged for me to see a doctor when they heard I had received no prenatal examinations so far, and they assured me there would only be a minimal charge for the doctor's services. My main concern was to get rid of my sinus infection and have my vaccination site checked out. It still bothered me considerably. As for being pregnant, that was a natural process and would take care of itself. Never before in my life had I considered that anything could go wrong. A case of blissful oblivion, for sure! And it never ceased to amaze me how much fuss was made over a pregnant woman, every place but at my in-laws.

The drawn-out process of writing home had been accomplished; it was a multiple page letter. The way I described my voyage and arrival had little in common with the actual occurrences, but I did not wish to worry my parents unnecessarily. I still had not told them that I was expecting a baby. There were so many months yet to go and it would have upset me too much to compare my reality with what I had written them on paper. Elaborating on the other extraordinary generalities of daily life here, so they could partially imagine it, was a good distraction for me. Explaining what just five cents could buy was a revelation and wonder: all local telephone calls, a cup of coffee (with free refills), and subway rides all day long if one did not emerge above ground. Unbelievable!

Travel between different states required no passport or ID. It took me several months to comprehend that before I retired my passport and ventured out without such an important document. In the food markets one was actually trusted to push a cart around, make one's own selections, take as long as one wanted, and then pay the cashier at the exit. After a movie Bill took me to one of the nearby saloons where the purchase of a beer was accompanied not only by free bread but with extra items suitable for a sandwich! It definitely took time before I got the nerve to take advantage of these offerings, for fear I would look like a pauper or thief. Describing all this was not easy and filled many pages, and I did not want to sound like a show-off. I could hear my father mumble: *"Papier ist geduldig"* (paper is patient), or, you can write what you want but that doesn't mean it's true. They were still, for the most part, battling hunger. I had promised my parents to send many a care package but now knew I could not make this promise come true. I had no money.

At home Bill's parents only subscribed to the German language newspaper. The help wanted ads therefore were very sparse and not of a category where one could hope for a decent job. This was his parents' world. They had nothing but German connections as their foundation. My father-in-law's own words were: "If anybody wants to talk to me, let them learn German." To bring an English language paper into the house was akin to being a traitor, but there were at least some decent job offers to be found there. Employment agencies were also a great lead. It was from one of those that Bill located a job in Brewster, New York. The job required a dairy man and an upstairs maid. We travelled by train for an interview, got a starting date the following week, and packed a suitcase and went.

When we arrived and wanted to settle into the accommodations provided, it turned out that the current couple did not want to vacate and were very quarrelsome. Given the circumstance, the superintendent gave us a bedroom and bath in the main house on a temporary basis. We were served breakfast in the kitchen off the butler's pantry. Bill's job was to milk about ten cows and keep the barn clean, along with other duties. My requirements were to make the beds all through the house. I hoped to high heaven nobody would suspect my pregnancy. My measly wardrobe provided nothing proper to wear as an upstairs maid. Short hemlines were the mode in Germany at the time. Here it was down to the ankles. I was given an old housedress as a uniform for servants.

The owner of the estate was a dentist and among his aspirations was to manipulate his name into the Social Register. Bill and I never got to meet the family. That was a good thing because the conditions became too unbearable and the other couple still refused to budge. With heavy hearts we again packed our suitcase and went back to Stewart Street. The interpretation of our return was that we probably were incapable, and Bill's parents feared we would fail at any other attempt. Lest we forget, we had found this ad in an English language paper, so no wonder it was no good. It seemed like Bill's parents had never really arrived in the United States.

It became a hellish hardship to return to the apartment before nightfall and face the condemnation hanging so heavily in the air. It made Bill search frantically on a daily basis for a job, any job, that would simultaneously give us accommodations and, therefore, our freedom—the freedom to fail or succeed.

The weather was still relentlessly cold with sleet and snow. It was during one of these icy evenings that my father-in-law was brought home with a broken arm. He had slipped on a subway grate and was both angry and in pain. It was difficult to tell which was more pronounced, the pain he was experiencing or the complete annoyance with himself. For now, a doctor had to be called to have his arm set. The commotion resembled a tragic comedy. My in-laws had the only telephone in the apartment house and this was one of the rare times it was used, to call in an emergency on their own behalf. During other times the phone was like the message center for all the other people living in the building. It made my mother-in-law feel like the all-knowing person, the town gazette.

The next few weeks were recuperation time for my father-in-law. Everyone was treading on eggshells, starting early in the morning, to determine which of his moods would rule the rest of the day. To him, to have anything derail one's physical condition and having to admit it seemed the ultimate insult to bear. I guess he saved his good moods only for the pinochle games at the German Club. From all indications he did not have any real sense of humor. Wanting to prove he held an equal or slightly superior stature to his buddies, he maintained a certain nervous guard that seemed never to leave him.

Close quarters at the apartment did not make the family close. Each one functioned on a separate island of the mind. I wondered what their last Christmas was truly like and if their hearts could open up and show a little emotion.

It made me think of Christmas 1946, the Christmas most memorable to me then and the last one I spent in Germany.

# CHAPTER 9

*Brooklyn*

**FROM BILL'S DIARY**
**Returning to Brooklyn**

It was good to be back in good old Brooklyn after being out of the country for almost one and a half years. I talked quite a bit to my parents about relatives but some of it they did not like to hear. I spoke even more about the conditions in Germany and they could not really grasp the situation. I was glad to see December 28 come. That was the day I went down to the pier to pick up Karola. She arrived on the *General RE Callan*, loaded with GIs. It turned out that my wife was seasick the whole ten-day trip across the Atlantic and now could barely make it down the gangplank into my arms. Those who could not make it had to go to Fort Hamilton or Ellis Island. Karola was fortunate enough to have a fellow CCD employee from Offenbach, Dr. Kalisher, inquire about her well-being aboard ship. At last there was somebody whom she knew.

This being a Sunday and the snow more than a foot high in New York City, we were lucky just to get to a subway station, much less see a taxi or bus anywhere. And so we took that long subway ride home to Stewart Street.

My parents, naturally, were anxious to see the girl I had married. I don't know what impression Karola got after trekking up those dimly lit flights of stairs. My wife was glad to sit down and rest in her condition, hoping that the next day would give her more strength. We had been promised by my mother that the living room would be all fixed up for us. It was the tail-end of the Christmas holiday and the decorated tree was still in that room, as had always been the custom. When my sister Margaret arrived later, she, too, gave Karola quite a critical going-over. I guess by now my wife weighed only about one hundred twenty-five pounds, and the main thing she needed was rest, love, and understanding, and then good food. Well, it seems that love and understanding were hard to come by in my family.

We eventually walked along many streets in Brooklyn with its shops filled with merchandise, and the transportation there was provided by comfortable, warm buses and trains. It was truly a treat for us, just having come from Germany. We felt proud to travel anywhere and buy the things we needed. It certainly was a joy to find no restrictions, as long as there were enough dollars in my pocket. My wife and I found much pleasure in just window-shopping or taking short trips by train to the city.

After it became apparent that Karola had not brought back lots of money, and especially when we told my parents the news that she was expecting, the atmospheric pressure shifted: the sooner we would move out the better for everybody. I had been taking a course at Delahanty (Fifteenth Street) for policemen and firemen and did quite well. Now that we had to be on our own quickly, this investment was down the drain and I had nothing to show for it. So, by the end of February we packed the suitcase and tried for a job on an estate near Purchase, New York. The living and working conditions, however, were not good, so after a week of this we returned to Brooklyn. My father gloried in the thought that we were dependent on him, so home became a hell for us, with many tears and heartaches. Every week I had given my parents my check for $20 from unemployment insurance and offered to double it if that would help ease the tension. But there was no compassion. I must admit I had never seen my parents so arrogant and heartless. Karola and I left every morning to destinations like the United Nations, the Empire State Building, Radio City, the theater, and even Coney Island and Prospect Park in Brooklyn. With these local excursions my wife became familiar with all the places I had already seen. At the same time, we were out of the house all day, returning in the evening. Sometimes we ate out but that was considered a waste of money.

One time we looked for a job in Brewster, New York. On the train coming home we happened to bump into Captain Lotz of *The Holbrook*, the ship that transported me back from Germany before Karola. What an odd coincidence! Interestingly, he had just paid a visit to his 400-acre farm in upstate New York.

1947 Bill returns from Allied occupation to Brooklyn

I shall never forget the disgruntled attitude displayed by my parents on my return from Germany. Homecoming was not greeted with the hearty welcome one would expect from parents. Having just experienced the distressful postwar conditions, I received criticism instead of any hint of empathy or solace. Not for a moment could I have visualized my parents this way—making home a living hell. It was pointed out to us that it was mother's influence that enabled preparation of the front room for our stay, temporarily of course, and we understood that only too well. I also never forgot what a calamity it was to my parents hearing of Karola's pregnancy. I resolved then and there not to trouble them ever again for anything. They are a frustrated people dreaming of some little home in the country far in the distance. We had to sleep in that thirty-five degree Fahrenheit living room for another week before we moved to New Jersey, where I secured a job through an agency in New York City.

## Leaving Brooklyn

On March 15, 1948 we finally left Brooklyn for Marlu Farms in Lincroft, New Jersey. A moving truck moved our few belongings like suitcases, a few wooden crates with dishes, a bed, a kitchen table, and two chairs. The whole moving enterprise cost us $28, and we even were included as passengers for the ride in the truck. At the farm we shared a large house with a couple named Czys. The house was two-family, with a separate entrance for each. The rooms were large and spacious, especially the bathroom with an old huge tub, which was a joy to use. Our neighbors minded their own business but otherwise were quite pleasant. Rudy Czys also worked for the farm's owner, whose name was Pollack, a hat manufacturer.

1948 First home after Brooklyn,
in two-family house

Rudy's wife, Virginia, had been in uniform overseas as a nurse and Rudy had been a prisoner of war, formerly with Anderson's Polish exiled army. Virginia marrying him made him a *male war bride*; Karola was an actual war bride. Rudy, being a deserter from the Polish Army, could not return to his native country, even as an American tourist. I believe he never saw his parents again. Virginia was quite a few years older than Rudy and married him while still overseas when he was a POW. About a half year later they left and bought a home on a six-acre farm nearby, where he ran a landscaping and gardening business. They never had children of their own but eventually adopted an orphaned boy.

For Karola and me it felt great living here at Marlu Farms. Even though we had no car, the Phillipses, our neighbors, were very friendly and helpful. They took Karola along shopping to Red Bank and were always so accommodating. My job was tough. I had to milk about thirty cows morning and night. The first day I had to play it cool. It was a big challenge to get into the swing of things again after being away from cows and the farm for so long. But I managed, getting up at 4 a.m., having breakfast at 7 a.m. and then working until noon. After that I was off until 4 p.m., when it was milking time again. This life in the country was first-rate. I had the use of an old truck, which I drove to work on the premises. My wages were $150 a month. Twice a week they provided three quarts of milk and two dozen eggs *on the house*. We got along fine with that, even if we could not afford a car. I guess my wife felt a little isolated at times, but otherwise she looked happy.

1948 Bill's first dairyman job

# CHAPTER 10

## Bill's Introduction to America

**FROM HIS DIARY:**

I remember it took a couple of trips from New York City to Oldenstadt by Otto Raethke to convince my father to come to the USA. The first time was in 1923 and then in the spring of 1928.

Otto and my father had sat on the same school bench in Oldenstadt when they were teenagers and full of mischief. After a year in Uelzen my father followed the same trade as his father in the carpentry business. Otto Raethke became a mason. At the age of nineteen he became quite involved in an amorous escapade and in 1912 somehow managed to leave the Old Country and come to the USA. At this time my father already had two years of army service behind him (1906-1908). When World War I broke out he enlisted immediately. After more than four years at the front he came home with tuberculosis and three artillery wounds. Following a month of recuperation he again worked in his father's carpentry shop.

I was born June 4, 1918. The years of inflation following the war caused endless, distressing hardship for most people. My mother had inherited about 11,500 marks when she married. This money became worthless and her dreams and ambitions shattered. Everybody had to make a new start, which seemed impossible with no work or jobs. The Versailles Treaty was hanging over Germany like an oppressive weight and purchase possibilities diminished, with no viable form of exchange in sight. Until the beginning of 1923 one could survive only by bartering. Baby carriages full of currency could not buy the necessities of life anymore. In this environment many young men with adventure in their hearts looked for greener pastures. At that time theft was a very common occurrence.

In the late 1920s my father worked for a man named Schulz in Uelzen for about forty-five marks a week. This money was just enough to keep our heads above water, and we belonged to the lucky ones. In such a climate most people were very disheartened. It was obvious that the demands of the Versailles Treaty, with steep reparations to be paid to the victors, would never allow Germany to get on its feet again. In such a demoralizing atmosphere it was easy for a man like Hitler to come to power.

In the spring of 1929, my grandfather advanced my father the necessary funds to sail to the USA. On May 30, 1929 my father left for Bremerhaven to board the *SS Albert Ballin* to New York City. He was thrilled to be aboard ship, which is evident from the one and only letter he sent from the ship, written to his friend Alfred Heuer while mid-ocean. Pop was met by his old school friend, Otto Raethke, and boarded with him in his furnished rooming house.

1929 Bill's father Wilhelm, passport photo

After settling in for a few weeks, my father worked his trade in his new surroundings. The wages were about $15 a day. That summer my father sweated more than he ever had in his entire life and many times he expressed the wish to return home.

As it turned out, he accumulated the required fare for my mother, brother, sister, and me, and ultimately, we all boarded the *SS Reliance* on October 18, 1929 bound for America. The twelve-day trip from Bremerhaven in the month of October seemed like a great adventure to me. Half the time I was seasick, however, and it seemed the dinner tables were half empty. The fare for my younger brother and sister was only $57.50, but I at eleven years old had to pay the adult fare of $115.

1929 Bill's mother Anny, passport photo

1929 Bill and siblings Johnny and Margaret, passport photo

I remember a couple of weeks before leaving Oldenstadt we auctioned off almost everything: all the furniture, beds, kitchen utensils, towels, bedspreads, linens, and so on. A few things like clothing, pictures, featherbeds and clocks were packed in wooden trunks and came with us aboard ship. My mother even brought some good potatoes. Onkel Heinrich hitched up a team of horses and we were ready to be brought to the Uelzener Railroad Station and from there to Bremerhaven. We made one stop first at the old schoolhouse to say goodbye to teacher Mohwinkel. He wrote a letter a few weeks after we arrived in New York that I still have today. When one left the Old Country, it was assumed that one would never return to friends and relatives in the old hometown. We arrived in the New World the day of the stock market crash. Nobody was there to greet us, so we had to go to Ellis Island, the Island of Tears (*Die Insel der Tränen*), for a day. What a disappointing experience that was. I felt rather protective toward my mother, but what does a boy of eleven know? It seems that my father and friends thought that nobody would be allowed off ship on a Sunday.

## Life and Impressions on the East Side of New York City

You can imagine the nervous state of my mother. The following day on Ellis Island, after physical examinations, as well as inspection of documents, everything was arranged and we went by car to our new home on the east side of Manhattan. Otto Raethke owned two three-story brick rooming houses side-by-side. We settled into a three-room basement apartment at 145 East Fifteenth Street. The rent was $10 a week. The change from living in a small country town with 732 inhabitants to the largest city in the world with seven million people, and living in the basement of a rooming house with hardly any sunlight or fresh air, really wrenched my nerves. My bedroom had no windows and adjoined the bathroom, which was also shared by other tenants in the building. There was no window for sunlight in the bathroom either. And the rooms always seemed to be filled with the smell of smoke.

My father was a dedicated *Skat* player back in Germany but here playing pinochle with the boys took its place. These games always went on till the early hours of the morning with Otto Raethke, Harry, and Reiner, who owned a bakery on Fifteenth Street and Third Avenue. We were practically sleeping next door to all this noise and smoke. The card playing was in the hope of winning a few dollars. It wasn't long before my nerves were again in high gear due to the tremendous contrast of the life I had known. Not familiar with a word of English, I started elementary school in the third grade with Miss Vanilla.

The first few hours were spent just writing my name in English. And oh how I rebelled against that *William* instead of *Wilhelm*. Arithmetic was a breeze for me, and I was fortunate that a German girl was there who could explain and translate for me.

After half a year of living in this *prison* of a rooming house, we finally moved by horse and wagon to Eighteenth Street on the east side. By this time we children felt that we had mastered the English language. It took a lot of persuasion by friends to get my father to move but he finally gave in. The apartment was on the top floor, the fifth, with five rooms. Now for the first time we had to buy all our own furniture, beds, kitchen utensils, and the like. Besides paying $42 a month rent, we paid for gas and electric as well. It took every penny we had and then some to get launched here. My father worked for a person from Denmark by the name of Hanson, who had a shop on East Sixteenth Street. The Depression was in full swing but my father always had work. He never learned the English language but somehow knew just enough to get by.

I believe we continued going to our former elementary school, so there was no problem with that. By this time I had skipped a couple of grades and was currently with students my own age. We went to church on East Nineteenth Street, where services were conducted in both German and English. It was also there that my brother and I were confirmed. I am sorry to say that my father never did go to church. We children had finally made some friends and participated in everything our American friends did. When I visited and sometimes had lunch with Scherman and Rosner, their parents would speak in Yiddish to me, knowing I had come from Germany. Besides roller-skating and playing ball in the street, we would use the school playground. On weekends we would sometimes go to Central Park on the L train or even go a little further to the Bronx Zoo. Many times during the month, when we had twenty-five cents, we would go to the movies at the Academy on Fourteenth Street.

For a quarter we could see six vaudeville acts besides a movie. Otherwise we spent ten cents for two or three features in the smaller movies. Before coming to this country I had only once seen a movie in Uelzen, a silent film with Charlie Chaplin on a small screen. In 1930-31, Fourteenth Street was the great Broadway for us, and First Avenue was *The Casbah* with its spices and aromas. The people here were from all countries in Europe and quite a few from India and Asia. We used to buy coffee here for as low as fifteen cents a pound. Many times we bought large rabbits from Canada for seventy-five cents each. The open market, with all its attractions, was very fascinating for me, but the hustle and bustle kept me on edge.

## We Move to Brooklyn, the Borough of Parks and Open Spaces

My father became a friend of the only co-worker in the carpenter shop who was from Schleswig-Holstein, Carl Obst. This man and his family lived in Brooklyn. It was he who convinced my father that living in Brooklyn was better and cheaper. This time it didn't take too much persuasion to get my father to move, since the bed bugs left him no peace at night.

So, in 1931, after one and a half years on Eighteenth Street of Manhattan's east side we moved to the top floor (third) at 14 Stewart Street, near Fourteenth Street in Brooklyn. Carl Obst and his family lived on the first floor. The two brick buildings were owned by Bescher, who was the landlord. The six apartments in each building were called railroad flats. The buildings were located right next to the BMT and elevated trains (the L). The whole move in itself is kind of vague in my memory. I do know that this was the first place where I felt free to breathe and get some sunshine. We really loved the open spaces in the Brooklyn location, in contrast to where we had lived in Manhattan. This was the borough of parks and churches.

In Brooklyn we made new friends in school and in the neighborhood. My brother was called Whitey and I was Dutchy. My sister had a good singing voice and in company she was not bashful to sing the latest hits. Here in Kings County we completed our elementary and high school education and followed our own desire without much guidance from our parents. Our parents joined the *Schleswig-Holstein Verein* (German Club) and by doing so were among German friends more often. The favorite meeting place was in the *Schwabenhalle* and occasionally in the Knickerbocker Hall in the Ridgewood section. It was also here that my parents celebrated their silver wedding anniversary with a band and over one hundred guests attending on November 15, 1941.

We children faithfully attended the local elementary school and later my brother and I went to Alexander Hamilton High School with a couple of boys from our street. Many times, we walked the thirty-five-minute stretch to school rather than spending the five cents for the L train. One winter day this turned out to be unfortunate for me because my ears froze! My sister went to a different high school, since Alexander Hamilton was an all-boys school.

At home in summer or winter we always felt quite comfortable. The hot water was heated by a gas burner and the apartment was kept warm with a ton and a half of coal per season. Coal at that time was $11 a ton and the $20 monthly rent did not change until 1954, when the new Puerto Rican landlord had to convert to heating with oil. Then the rent was raised to $50 per month and never changed until my parents left for the Ivy House Nursing Home in New Jersey. We actually treasured that nice big stove in the kitchen. I guess it reminded us of the Old Country where we usually found plenty of wood that didn't cost us anything. My father always had a job and that was our capital. All through the Depression years of the 1930s we never felt deprived of anything.

In our building lived English, Irish, German, and Italian families, and these groups made up the whole neighborhood. In the early thirties, when Prohibition was still on the books, the Italian family pressed grapes and made wine in the cellar, while we made beer and whisky. The hops for the beer were imported from Germany. We had five-gallon crocks and a bottle capper, plus everything else necessary to have an adequate supply. I remember on rare occasions in the cold winter months, some of the capped bottles would pop. But for many years we were satisfied with our brew. The fine copper still remained in my possession for many years and not until 1960 did I finally get rid of it.

Everyone at 14 Stewart Street had his own bin in the cellar with coal, wood, booze, trunks, stools, and other equipment. In the summertime we went through the cellar into the small back yard, where we had a little flower garden. We also had many a card game there in the summer with the Matthews, the Frascos, and us. Our favorite walk on a sunny Sunday was to Evergreen Cemetery, where my father would read his German paper. On weekends we spent many hours at Highland Park. There in winter an ice skating rink was available, as well as good sledding. During summer we made good use of the parallel and horizontal bars in the park, and it was refreshing just to walk around the reservoir.

School was rather uneventful for me. The first year in high school I was in Arista (honor society) but in the following years I barely passed. I didn't mind being in school but I surely looked forward to those three months of summer vacation. In the early 1930s many months were spent at Coney Island Beach. A nickel fare would get us there and we'd spend all day having a great time.

# CHAPTER 11

*My Paternal Grandparents*

**I DID NOT MEET MY** paternal grandparents until the age of six. By then my parents had finally been able to move into an apartment of their own for the first time. Until we were actually living together as a family, I was not acquainted with my father either, so no bonding of any kind had taken place. I felt he was like a total stranger, but now I had to abide by his rules and regulations and forge a new relationship with my mother. She was no longer there just for me. She had to answer to this person before I could even speak with her. Having married into a lower class than the one she was born into, she had to forget about wearing jewelry, hats, or gloves. The latter two items were for practical purposes only, when weather conditions called for them. She was now a worker's wife with no frills allowed. More than anything I missed her parents, my true Opa and Oma.

My father came from the lower echelon of blue-collar workers with a hand-to-mouth existence and very strict upbringing. His parents were serious people, which the severity of that period reinforced. No laughter, humor, or jokes. It would have been considered a mockery of the daily grind, so they just plowed through. The first time I met my new grandparents was when my parents had to go out of town on an errand. I felt very strange and awkward with my grandmother. She had a stern expression and never smiled. In contrast, my grandfather, with his clear blue eyes, reflected the goodness of a pure soul. He was a quiet man and the one who would lift me onto his lap. In that protective haven I felt secure. It was so peaceful there with him and most of all I felt he was sincere, caring, and trustworthy.

1914 Karola's father Wilhelm Friedmann (lft.), his parents Margarethe and Leonhard, and his sisters Mariechen (top lft.) and Sophie

He would read the paper while I watched my grandmother bustle about the small kitchen. On the table I could observe a little green frog in a jelly jar climbing to the top on his cute little ladder. *Frosch* tried to reach the holes in the paper cover of the jar whenever a freshly caught fly would be fed to him. What great pest control via organic recycling! I felt quite special when I was given permission by my grandmother to water the fuchsia plants on the balcony. The apartment was a fourth-floor walk-up, consisting of a tiny entrance hall, small kitchen, narrow bedroom, and a small living room, where nobody ever really spent time or felt comfortable. In the winter it was not heated. Life was confined to the kitchen and the cold bedroom. The toilet did not deserve such a proper name. One had to go with a key half a flight down; behind the door was a wooden seat with a hole in the middle and a wooden cover. No flushing was necessary—everything just fell below by force of gravity—and little newspaper squares were there for wiping purposes. This was usually a good time to catch up on old news, obituaries, or ads. Behind the seat was a wide pipe through which resounded the blessings from the apartments above.

The closeted space containing the *throne* deserves detailed description simply because of its primitive characteristics. A little window allowed fresh air in, but with it circulated huge flies resembling flying blueberries, particularly during the warmer months. It was a major embarrassment when someone had to use the other facility on the same landing. There was no way to muffle the sporadic orchestral wind tones. At night one had to exit the apartment with a flashlight, since there was no hint of illumination in the entire stairwell. This venture preceded the total darkness encountered at the toilet itself. Flashlights were expensive and the batteries didn't always work. For nighttime nature calls there was a chamber pot under every bed. How awkward and cringe-worthy it was to carry specimens down the staircase . . . while also aiming the flashlight. What if you met a visitor or another tenant along the way? Hygiene and dignity were difficult to maintain, especially if a family member was ill.

*Grossvater* (Grandfather) Friedmann had a job as a machinist in a large tool factory about a half-hour walk from home. He would leave very early in the morning because he received extra pay for firing up the furnace, then stayed all day until late afternoon. On one winter evening he slipped on an iron grate and broke his thigh bone in two places. Even after the bones were set and healed, he walked with the aid of a cane and was regarded as an invalid. He had quite a noticeable limp and it was so painful to watch him walk. I felt great sadness for my grandfather, particularly because my grandmother was forever harping on how stupid it was for him to fall in the first place. He became increasingly withdrawn and eventually lost his job. His meager workmen's compensation could barely sustain a scanty living for the two of them. Constant worry about the next day made it difficult for him to focus on nourishment or derive any enjoyment from his meals when he came to the table.

The atmosphere in their apartment became so depressing that I no longer had any desire to visit them. There was nothing to talk about. What could a child say, anyway, to bring a change to the situation? My father then became the intermediary. He would go shopping for food and other necessities. Eventually my grandfather became so ill that his system could no longer absorb necessary nutrients. He was hospitalized and diagnosed with cancer of the stomach. The disease had progressed so rapidly that there was no possibility for a successful operation. He was transferred from the hospital to a long-term care facility of sorts, similar to hospice. He was in such pain that only morphine could keep him comfortable. Many times, my father would take on night-watch duty by his bedside to relieve the nurses and keep the costs down. Grandmother would sit with him during the day, but then after a while he did not recognize anyone anymore. My dear, beloved, sweet grandfather, Leonhard Friedmann, born February 2, 1868, passed away on May 31, 1931 at sixty-three years of age. This was the first death of anybody I had known. It was so hard for me to grasp that he was no longer there, he in whose presence I could feel so safe and serene. I was then eight years, five months, and two days old.

The day of my grandfather's funeral I spent with my mother's parents (my favorite Opa and Oma). As was the custom, I was to read from the Bible during the ceremony. Children were not to be present at graveside. It was for adults only. Afterward everybody went back to their respective homes except widowed *Grossmutter* (Grandmother) Friedmann, who went for a few days' stay with her eldest daughter. This was my Tante Mariechen, my father's older sister. She was the only one with a larger, more modern apartment, which had an extra bed. Also in the household were Mariechen's sons, my cousins Karl and Rudi Steinkrug.

Both of our families lived in the same town, Offenbach, and just a few streets apart. But they might as well have been worlds apart. There was never a big get together as a clan, which is so hard to understand today. No one came visiting us either, since my father could scare anyone away with his severe and inhospitable nature. Yet his behavior was more about pride in who he was and not revealing how poor our circumstances were.

Now that Grossmutter Friedmann was all alone, she became reclusive, quarrelsome, and obstinately moody. I dreaded the many errands I now had to run for her, never knowing in what state of mind I would find her, but I did them in memory of my dear departed grandfather. My Tante Mariechen worried constantly about her mother's health and continually urged her to have a checkup. Her worries were confirmed; my grandmother had breast cancer. To save her life a radical mastectomy of one breast was necessary. The years following her operation were quite sad and frustrating for her, even though tests showed she was in remission. It became increasingly oppressive to be in my grandmother's presence. I wanted so much to cheer her up, yet her lifelong negative attitude could not be changed. Then came 1939 and the beginning of World War II.

Everything now was about preparedness of the home front. The world as my grandmother had known it in her narrow circle had crumbled. No complaints of hers would change anything one iota.

She had no more control over the circumstances of her life. In early 1940 Rudi and Karl Steinkrug had to join the Army and Marines, respectively. That was another separation and loss. By then we had air raids and bombings, and spent many hours in bunkers, the huge buildings we had not figured a use for years earlier. Grandmother's cancer had returned, and a second operation was necessary. After my working hours, if no air raid was in progress, I would visit her. These were the only times we actually grew a little closer. She would be glad to have a few hours of company and even talked woman-to-woman. Unfortunately, the operation had not produced promising results. Over many months she hovered between life and death, until Margarete Friedmann (née Beck), born February 25, 1871, passed away on December 18, 1942. The timing spared her knowledge of the destruction of her apartment in an air raid.

Grossmutter Friedmann's funeral had to be postponed several times. Air raids caused the delay, and the removal of rubble from destroyed houses took time. There was no means of communication with the proper authorities or of reaching the minister to set a date. At any moment there could be another bomb attack. It was my father who made certain, after a week, that there was some finality. If there was a ceremony of any kind, that remained unknown but doubtful; it was constantly a run for survival.

✳ ✳ ✳

A document image from the *Familienstammbuch* (family tree book) registers an entry my father made about his own grandfather, Kaspar Friedmann.

Occupation: *Zimmermann* (carpenter)
Religion: Catholic
Date of Birth: June 21, 1840, in Seligenstadt/Main (near Offenbach/Main).
Exact Date of Death: unknown, however the place of death is shown as Sunnol Gleen, California, America.

All my father knew about his grandfather (and this by word of mouth) was that he had left his wife and children back in Germany, sailed to the country rumored to be where milk and honey flows to find a better life and have his family follow as soon as he had found the financial means. The only thing they received after a while was notification of his death. The letter was somehow lost. If the timing of his departure for a better future coincided with the Gold Rush, it is unknown to me. All that remained was the terrible life for his family he left behind, and the abundant shame and sniping regarding his *convenient disappearance.* Gossips surmised he could not cope with his responsibilities; he was chasing fortune; he was a loser and nobody wanted to rub elbows with that type. Or so the litany went.

As I write these pages in the early days of June 1999 I am wondering if, by computer magic and Internet today, more could be found out. I tried earlier, in 1946, to unearth more information but my inquiries came back unanswered. There is no such place as Sunnol Gleen in California. Maybe it was a ghost town. I, as this man's great-granddaughter, would be fascinated to unravel some of this story, the voyage, the troubles, the end. And is there a grave somewhere in the dust of California? As with so many mysteries of history, I may never find out.

# CHAPTER 12

*Survival During the War*

**AIR RAIDS WERE THE NORMAL** condition during the war years. In anticipation of these formerly unimaginable horrors, each house on the street was now connected through the cellars. Houses were built in such a manner that they touched side by side, with no dividing space. On each side of the abutting cellars a crawl space was opened and only slightly cemented shut, with a sledgehammer lying on each side of the escape hatch. If there was a really big hit, it was possible to get out via this tunnel. Our house, Lilistrasse 45, had already been fire-bombed late in 1939, with the attic and top floor apartments damaged by fire and water. It was then we started to become gypsies. We first took shelter with my mother's sister, Amalie Lutz (Tante Mali) on Bettinastrasse.

But the three of us could not all stay there. My mother went to stay with her parents, and I stayed with my Tante Greta on Friedrichstrasse until that, too, was bombed. My father stayed for a while with his sister, Tante Mariechen. Not only were we refugees without a change of clothes, but we had huge difficulty acquiring food ration coupons and finding food. As much as one person wanted to help another, no one was welcome anywhere any longer. Life began to be subhuman, not even considering a means to maintain cleanliness. Personal hygiene as one had known it, even with cold water flats, was now an individual dilemma to be dealt with in the spirit of every man for himself.

My mother had zero ability to run or walk quickly to the bunker when those damn sirens flared, given her serious ulcerated varicose veins, but her condition secured her a permit of occupancy for a lower bunk bed in the nearest bunker for every night. At least she could look forward to some repose, as primitive as this was. I had the same privilege in the bunkers because I was her designated caregiver. My father had to fend for himself. During the day he had to arrive as punctually as possible at his job. We became superb actors. How we managed to make do one more night for the glory of the Third Reich! Those enemies would not break our morale. Everything now became more rationed than before; as Hermann Goering (a primary architect of the Third Reich Nazi police state) declared: *Kanonen anstatt Butter* (canons instead of butter). It was easy for him to talk. Even if we may have had money to afford a little butter there was none to be had. The black marketeers never suffered, of course, and Hermann was fat enough.

We waited to see if he would reduce in girth. In reality, we had to feed the men on all fronts, and the POWs as well, and the only front poorly fed and clothed was the home front.

Appeals were now going to the population owning autos, motor bikes, and especially side cars. It was more confiscation than appeal, an order from the very top. Farmers not only saw their sons drafted but their horses, too. There was no guarantee of having anything returned. It was viewed as your pride and honor to give, give, give. A wrought iron fence found at a fancy villa on the outskirts of town would be removed for the same reason. Church bells had to come down from steeples and be melted down for canons. Yet in many cases it had not been anticipated that this would require manpower and special equipment, as well as transportation to factories. Many church bells were consequently saved, still sitting near the entrance of the sanctuary, or even left hanging in the tower. The church where I was confirmed, Schlosskirche, had become a ruin. I had so hoped to be married in that church someday.

As the war accelerated there was no end in sight and one became more lost in hopeless resignation. Why would the outside world not see through Hitler's bluff and put an end to this madness? He was still declaring that the Third Reich would exist for 1,000 years, while every realistic person could see we were winning ourselves to death on all lines of battle. Hundreds of our young men fighting did not know they had no home left to return to. Two of those young men were my cousins Rudi and Karl. Not only was their former home destroyed (an entire block bombed to dust) but their mother, my Tante Mariechen, died in that night of terror, along with most residents there. Days later my Onkel Rudolf, who was with the police department, was able to organize excavator machines in order to dig into the former cellar/tunnel where they would have sat in the shelter. My father and I were there, as well, to support Onkel Rudolf and to make positive identification. We all got sick not only from the stench of bomb chemicals, but in the process of trying to gather body parts that may have constituted a whole person. Everything was covered with gray dust and the bodies and parts appeared like limp, boneless rags. My aunt, Marie Steinkrug (nee Friedmann), born 1892 (approximately), died March 18, 1944, in such a horrible way while her sons were still fighting, one on the eastern front and one somewhere at sea. In a way it was a blessing that Grossmutter Friedmann had been spared from knowing her eldest daughter died like this.

Onkel Rudolf, my father, Reverend Winkelmann, and I

gathered at the new cemetery outside Offenbach. Foreign Polish laborers were carrying a raw pine box; maybe Tante Mariechen was in there? Just as they started to lower the casket into a mass grave, there was a surprise air attack of low flying planes with machine guns sputtering. We all fell to the ground, which was the only thing we could do. I never felt my feet so far removed from my body. I did not dare even blink, feeling total terror. The actual target was the nearby train tracks. It took us a while to realize we were all still alive, except my poor Tante.

Quickly, before any more attacks could occur, the Polish forced laborers dropped the primitive pine box in the massive hole and ran as fast as their legs could carry them out of the cemetery. Reverend Winkelmann mounted his dilapidated bike (the tires were wound with old elastic bandages) and left. The rest of us had to walk the long way home. Home now happened to be an assigned space in a leather goods factory, very cramped, but at least there was a bathroom. The wartime shortages of materials had stopped production in this little factory, so the space had to be made available for us bombed out individuals. The owner of the place hated to share anything and was known for his greed, but he was a devout Catholic. He put us under all kinds of restrictions—we, who had already been restricted in every conceivable way. One had the constant feeling we were sheep being led to slaughter, while his family still had not suffered loss of any kind.

Utter dismay registered on the owner's face as we returned with yet another person, Onkel Rudolf. But there was nothing he could do about evicting him or any of us; these were orders from high up. Onkel Rudolf was in deep shock, sinking deeper by the minute. He became almost a ghost of himself with unspeakable grief affecting his mind: he thought I was Mariechen. His head fell onto my shoulders with great sobs wrenching his body. I had never felt such a deep understanding of sorrow before. Since I was always the youngest child looking up to and living with the grownups, it was assumed I was able to handle everything. I had never experienced emotions like this in any of my elders. In his mixed-up state, Onkel wanted to make love to me! I had to shake him violently and bring him back to reality, reminding him I was his niece and not his wife. He finally snapped out of his stupor. He came back to himself and could not believe what he had imagined and asked of me. But now he also realized the horrific finality of becoming a widower under unfathomable circumstances. The hardest task yet ahead was to contact Karl and Rudi with the tragic news of their mother's death. Perhaps they could get a short furlough home?

With this on his mind Rudolf left to blunder back to Offenbach. With the police headquarters now underground he made it his temporary home and sent field telegrams out to the boys. We saw Onkel Rudolf only once more. That was when Karl came for a week's stay with us and we had to go together to visit the mass grave where his mother lay. Overwhelming sorrow and sadness descended on Karl. When he encountered the destruction of his hometown and former neighborhood, along with the displacement of friends and neighbors, he could not wait to return to his submarine. His beloved mother was gone forever. His father had found a woman friend in the meantime and his brother Rudi was now missing in action on the eastern front. Karl had nothing left and turned bitter with the torment of attempting to make sense of this brutal reality. We had no additional ration points to feed him, or even ourselves for that matter, and no creature comforts to offer. After the next air raid, he just up and left and went back to the war.

# CHAPTER 13

## *Tante Greta*

**IN THE LATE 1930S MY** mother's sister Tante Greta decided to take advantage of Hitler's offer: every German worker could own a car. Accomplishing that goal required a specific process. Booklets were distributed to interested persons and five-mark value stamps were to be pasted inside. When the full total of 500 marks was reached, the car, a Volkswagen, could be ordered through proper channels and procedures.

Tante Greta was overwhelmingly ecstatic about the whole concept. It gave her a positive outlook, anticipating car ownership, driving lessons, and independent travel. Such extravagances were not available to the average working person, especially not to a woman. At the time she had been widowed for years. Onkel Alwin died of colon cancer and she had nursed him throughout the ordeal with undying love and devotion for five years. Now she was alone. The hope for this car was her dream, held aloft by steadfast confidence in Adolf Hitler's assurance. He had depicted a great future for Germany and she saw herself becoming part of it.

Then the war came. All those who already owned a Volkswagen

were ordered to donate it to the mighty cause. The automobiles and anything else on wheels, including motor bikes and bikes with side cars, were drafted, painted in camouflage colors, and now belonged to the war machine. Tante Greta's booklet was only half filled with stamps, so she put it aside for the uncertain future of her vision. She kept working at her job as a Red Cross nurse for the home front.

As the war progressed bombs fell all around us. All of our family members were bombed out repeatedly and had to seek out different shelters. I know for a fact Tante Greta had that stamp booklet always on her person, along with other remaining so-called valuables. She was clinging to a dream because, at that time, what else was there? With surrounding destruction, desperation, and sleep and food deprivation, that vision was steadily descending downhill into the bomb craters. With gravely shaken beliefs, attacks everywhere by Hitler, and the home front increasingly a scene of annihilation, Tante Greta's life outlook gradually shifted to thoughts of a quiet and painless way out. Earlier she had so firmly believed that her Addie (her pet name for Hitler) would make everything right. Her child-like naive faith soon vanished, which was a troubling change to see in her. As a nurse she had gained access to medications. I could only surmise what would provide an out for her if things became unbearable. I know where she kept her *dream* and there must also be the *out*.

Since Tante Greta had no children, I often kept her company, living with her whenever I could through all the various moves to different shelters, setting up a new place to live until that, too, was bombed. We were survivors so far and survival mode was now geared more to the next hour, or maybe the next day, or perhaps even the next week, if we were really fortunate.

I was steadily driven by how and where to find her stash of pills that she had mentioned in an unguarded moment. My admired and beloved aunt should not fall victim to the lunacy created by Hitler. She was my role model as far back as I could remember. I always looked up to her. Whatever she did, said, or wore had the aura of a certain elegance and class about it, even if she was in the very plainest attire. She had seen better times as a concert singer when she met Onkel Alwin, a musician and *Kappellmeister* (conductor); they were married before he joined the army in World War I—called the war to end all wars.

circa 1911 Tante Greta

circa 1911 Tante Greta's husband Alwin Goerner

Later in the war, she had been allotted another living quarter, the third after forced eviction from the ruined remains in Friedrichstrasse and then Waldstrasse. This one had a bathroom and a small former dressing room that were part of a large and spacious apartment. The bathroom became her kitchen, the small dressing room (walk-in closet) her combination bedroom and living room, and the rest of the apartment on Karlstrasse was divided between two other families. I occasionally visited her from where my parents and I were ordered to live at the moment. She had managed to make her restricted quarters quite functional and attractive, considering the circumstances and possibilities. One of the electrical outlets still worked and she had a little kettle; everything was cooked or heated with that. An old ironing board placed over the bathtub served as a table.

Finally, in 1945 the collapse of the Third Reich was upon us. The Russians occupied the east all the way to Berlin. News of Hitler's demise spread through all the destroyed territories and finally to us in the west, which became the American military occupied zone.

At that point Tante Greta's dream shattered with terminal cruelty. I had to find the *stuff* she obviously had saved. While she one day went to beg and plead for some groceries at a nearby makeshift distribution center, I had the opportunity to search for it. I came upon an old eyeglass case and inside there it was, a little glass vial with some capsules; and neatly folded to miniature size, the booklet of stamps, her *Volkswagen Dream*. Contents of the vial took three flushes to make them vanish.

Tante Greta never let on about the disappearance of *her way out* but took life as it came, one day at a time. The last occasion I saw her was during my visit to Offenbach in 1957 when we spent a most happy overnighter, giggling like kids, remembering the better days. What an era she lived between World War I and World War II. She had always projected a warm sincerity and uplifting spirit, a gift to those fortunate enough to be in her presence. I still have her engagement ring, which was finally passed down to me as the youngest niece. Her and Onkel's wedding rings have also united after all these years in my small jewelry box. What miracles of survival!

# CHAPTER 14

*Thoughts of My Mother*

**AFTER MANY DECADES AND FINALLY** writing about bygone history, it strikes me I had not taken note of certain dates in relation to my start in life. The beautiful picture of Tante Greta on Christmas 1922 was taken only five days before my birth on December 29, 1922. What the mood was in the Max and Klara Schroeder (the parents of my mother and Tante Greta) household I can only barely imagine. My mother was still living there, my father was living with his parents, awaiting my birth, and both were hoping for any opportunity to get an apartment of their own. Four years after World War I, with major inflation underway, one could say it was the worst of times and a cold, bleak December.

1922 Christmas, Karola's favorite aunt, Tante Greta

circa 1908 Karola's mother Karoline (ctr.) b.1899,
aunts Greta (rt.) b.1890 and Amalie (lft.) b. 1887

I wonder if Tante Greta and Tante Amalie, the oldest of
the three Schroeder daughters, were looking forward to my
impending birth, given that their youngest sister was the mother-
to-be. Was this a happy situation or was there discord regarding
social differences and financial position? History is shrouded
in silence, yet my mind so often wonders and wanders back. To
not know my father until the age of six leaves the prior years
cloaked in mystery. And the fact that it was only then that I met
my paternal grandparents remains puzzling. Though they lived

just around the corner at Goethestrasse 71, how close yet how far apart they were physically and socially.

Reflection brings me back to thoughts about my mother. Each year spring in particular brings her spirit so near to me. Springtime meant Mother's Day was coming. My earliest memories of this occasion were closely entwined with her agony over what she would do or give to her mother, my Oma. Unlike her two older sisters, no fancy bouquets from the florist were within her means. She would take me into her confidence and we'd pray for beautiful weather to gather fern and early violets in the nearby woods. On this annual trip we felt like close buddies and yet so humble. Would Oma like the flower offering? What about my own Mama? I had inherited the same struggle with the very same subject, since I was taught so early the true meanings of the heart. What bothered me already as a child of six, seven, and so on was the sense of obligation to do something showy, when in fact it did not matter the size or worth of the gift. Hugs and kisses were not even on the radar. How sad. I have learned so differently here in America.

1917 Karola's mother Karoline at age 18

When I left Germany, I had not told my parents of my great expectations: I was to become a mother myself! My leaving was sad enough for them. The big trip to America occupied my heart and being united with my Bill wiped out all other concerns.

Once my mother and I were reunited with my father and lived together on Lilistrasse and I was old enough to cross the streets by myself, it became my duty to act as messenger between home and my mother's parents, my Oma and Opa. However, I did this very often with a heavy heart. When my mother had received some homemade prepared goods from Oma, my proud father would reject this kind gift with bitter tirades, and I was the one who had to bring it back. Inside and outside I was crying all the way to Domstrasse with the items, thinking of how I was to return them, and with what message? And I had to report back at home how it went. I could never forget how adults could be so cruel. I felt like the sacrificial lamb, this little child, me, so young at seven or eight years of age. Many times I lied after returning from such a trip, having left the contribution on the stairs outside Oma's entrance and hoping a beggar would help himself to it. Or hopefully Frau Mueller, the cleaning woman who lived a flight up, would take it to flesh out her lean pantry. I didn't have the heart to tell my mother the truth, hoping Oma would not feel sad. If my dear Opa ever found out, I never knew. He was a gentleman and would never mention it; silent waters ran deep on Domstrasse and *never* on Lilistrasse.

Anticipating everybody's emotional state at any given time of day trained my gut feelings early on. I knew exactly what the overriding mood was by entering a room and tuning in to the occupants. The density of the atmosphere informed me.

I will never know how my mother made the transition from a relatively good life to one of daily crisis, though the stresses of each day, combined with her station in life, could explain much of it. She had a lifelong problem with ulcerated varicose veins, was subjected to verbal and psychological abuse, faced the constant agony of stretching one mark, and dealt with a myriad of difficulties on a regular basis. I remember when she was unable to manage the stairs, she would send me to the grocery store across the street for some broken eggs (I was given a small bowl for that), or one eighth pound of margarine. I could feel exactly how welcome I was in the store for such an order. In my recollection I still feel embarrassment for the unsuspecting grocer, having to cut the one-pound cube into hopefully not more than one eighth. Much oleo stuck to the knife and how could he sell the rest of the mangled mess to anybody else? Such concerns and worries should never be thrust upon a child. But that was how it was and my assistance with such errands was a help to my mother.

After my arrival in the USA in December 1947, my first Mother's Day came on May 9, 1948. So, early in April it was time to select and send a card to Mama, telling her from one mother-to-be to a grandmother-to-be: *Happy Mother's Day!*

# CHAPTER 15

*Twins on Mother's Day!*

**BILL'S VERSION**

From his diary:

On Saturday, May 8, there were all signs that Karola was about to deliver. That night, about 1 a.m., I had to try to get to a phone and call Dr. Podell, a doctor in Red Bank, New Jersey. Neither we nor our neighbors, the Czyses, had a telephone. The nearest neighbors with a phone were the Phillipses. Their house was about a half mile away and they were sound asleep. Approximately an hour later I managed to reach Dr. Podell. We had never been to his office nor had we ever met him before. He knew approximately where we lived because he had delivered a baby to another Marlu Farms family. He volunteered to come out at the time. I was to take the old truck to the highway with the high beams on so he would know where to turn. When he finally arrived and had examined Karola he told me to boil plenty of water and get lots of towels and newspaper. I guess he expected a delivery soon. When by 5 a.m., however, things had not changed much, the doctor phoned for an ambulance and we all went to Riverview Hospital in Red Bank. About two hours later Dr. Podell came into the lobby, his apron full of blood, and told me that I was the father of twins. I was so glad to hear that Karola and the twins were okay and felt that everything would be fine. I was not allowed to see my wife at that time, so I was picked up by the Czyses and brought home. After that I saw Karola every day. She was so overjoyed to see little Margaret and Billy. The room at the hospital was also quite cheerful, overlooking the waterfront. After nine days she was finally released from the hospital and we were all driven home by our neighbor.

1948 Riverview Hospital, where twins were born

Now we were living on Marlu Farms as a family. We were very fortunate to have such a wonderful home where the rooms were large with plenty of light and the heat could be regulated. Great care was necessary for the twins, especially during the first two to three months. They were born a month and a half premature and weighed only four and a half pounds each at birth. After being home for about two days, Karola was exhausted and completely down with her nerves. At this time Mrs. Phillips was a tremendous help. I also engaged a Mrs. Ross, recommended by Dr. Podell, for twelve days to look after the twins from 7 p.m. to 7 a.m.

The cost was only $12 a day then. She was a great asset! The hospital bill was about $100, and the doctor charged $80 for the delivery. Life in Lincroft, New Jersey during these summer months was very happy and pleasant. The babies made rapid progress and the parents got more sleep.

## Karola's Version

On May 7, 1948, the weather was getting really warm, and I was beginning to feel very tired. My ankles, wrists, and fingers were swelling up so much and I blamed it on the extra time and energy expended on domestic projects: giving the living room floor a second coat of varnish and sewing receiving blankets on Virginia's treadle sewing machine. Extensive exertion was supposedly a no-no for a pregnant gal but, other than the few preparations I had made, I felt not yet ready for the birth. According to calculations the due date would not be until the end of June or the beginning of July. I had plenty of time, I thought.

I went to bed early on that Saturday evening. I could not get into a comfortable position, as my back was aching. I must have dozed off and on; it was not a restful sleep. I kept dreaming about a stomachache. My persistent dreams were getting more and more real and I had to wake up Bill. He thought it was something I ate but I was not so sure. It must be what labor pains are supposed to be. The pains did not go away. "Please, Bill, call a doctor in Red Bank," I asked him.

There was not a telephone in the house, so he had to go and wake up the Phillips family, the only people with a phone for far and wide. They were a half mile away and now it was almost one o'clock in the morning on a Sunday. But before he got dressed, my Bill had to, of all things, shave. I tried telling him I was in agony but he had to shave first.

Before he left, he woke up Virginia next door to stay

with me until he got back. She had been a nurse in the service and she could be of assistance. But lo and behold, Virginia knew *Nothin' 'bout birthin' babies, Miss Scarlett!* So we were two dummies, knowing nothing about this whole business and my water broke, another calamity I knew nothing about. After what seemed like an eternity, Bill finally came back, thank the Lord, with a doctor. His name was Dr. Podell. He took one look at the situation and gave Virginia and Bill orders to boil water, bring towels and newspaper, and make haste. In a schoolmaster manner he reprimanded Bill for giving the impression over the telephone that I was suffering from what he understood to be a migraine headache and nausea, and consequently he had not brought his special bag. Now I was surrounded by three people, one of them the expert. The latter tried to speak German a little, thinking I might not understand him, and was proud that some of his Yiddish was like German slang. My labor pains had progressed, with the doctor telling me that any moment there would be a baby, but as time went by nothing happened. I was trying so hard to follow all his wise instructions. At this point the doctor sent Bill over to the neighbors to call for an ambulance and give directions how to get to our place.

After a long wait the ambulance arrived. The assistants secured me to a stretcher and literally had to slide me down the staircase ever so slowly. I could feel every bump. And to think I was in the same blasted nightgown that had caused me terrible embarrassment on my day of arrival in Brooklyn! Nobody cared. I was now in the ambulance with the doctor holding my hand and telling me, "Don't bear down, don't push!"

The sirens were wailing; I could not help but feel important with those sirens sounding loudly because of *me*!

At this early hour! And it was perfectly alright! I kept telling the doctor that I was getting very tired, my heart felt very tired, and that I had *never* felt so *tired*. He reassured me that all would be fine, we were almost at the hospital, and he would see to it that I get the best care.

I felt that so far I had the most attention I ever received in my entire life. Even the birds gave us their most brilliant songs and the lilac bush by the house was so fragrant. I inhaled the scent just prior to being loaded into the ambulance. Now the fragrance had changed to the anesthetic and the doctor made me count backwards from ten. *How stupid does he think I am? But, he is wonderful, he doesn't hate me because I am German, and how lucky I am to be in his care . . . ten . . . nine . . . eight . . . What a cute little boy, he is so tiny . . . Well, wait, doctor . . . there is another one . . . Oh, it's a girl . . . .*

If I could just think a little clearer, seems like some lady had twins and the nurses are having a debate over who is cuter, the boy or the girl. I am so exhausted. I have to relax. I will see who that is later. My eyelids are so heavy, can't lift them to see. Ah, here I go for a ride. Hey, my bed has wheels. How great!

Such a good sleep I had, waking up in a sunny room, wondering what happened. Where was I in my life? Oh, yes, about to have a baby. Did I have the baby yet? One way to find out, yes, I can see my feet, it must really have happened. Now, where is everybody? What about the baby? Is it okay? Nobody's here, nobody's coming . . . They don't want to tell me the bad news. There must be something wrong.

*I have to close my eyes again; resting is so delicious. There is this bright light and such radiance coming from the doorway. Have I gone to Heaven? Am I seeing God in His glory? I have to focus better.*

It was Bill, pale but grinning from ear to ear, telling me that we had twins! A boy and a girl!

"How are they?" I asked him.

"They are cute, tiny."

"Yes, but are they alright? Healthy?"

"Yes, yes, the doctor says they are fine."

"Can I see them?"

"No, they are in an incubator."

"Oh, my God! There is something wrong with them and nobody's telling me! What is an incubator?"

"It is like a warming oven, since they are so low in weight, and this way, they can be monitored much better."

"But when can I see them?"

"After a twenty-four-hour period, the nurse will bring them to you tomorrow morning. The doctor will see you later, too. He's so happy for us. Now, you've got to take it easy. We are actually *famous* here for having twins on Mother's Day, and I have got to go home and change. The Phillipses are waiting downstairs for me. I will be back later," he said, with several kisses.

I wanted to ponder about all that happened in those few hours on May 9, 1948, but after another sound sleep. I fell promptly back to a contented slumber until later when Bill came back again.

I went in and out of dreaming, one moment still on the ship, and the ship not landing. I dreamed I was not allowed to enter America and would have to go back to Germany.

When I awoke, the next realization settled over me that I had just become a mother! I had two babies. Now I was waiting to feel like a mother, but nothing happened. Maybe when I saw them and held them? Bill and I were now parents forever. I didn't trust happiness to overcome me yet. I needed to *see* and *know* that those two tiny babies were really okay. Then, I would be overwhelmingly happy and give thanks to God for this miracle.

Another realization hit me: *not only do I have two babies, but they are United States citizens*! I was therefore the only foreigner in my new little family. I have to wait five years before I can even apply for citizenship. Never mind, I have to float on my joyful thoughts and wait for Bill to come back later.

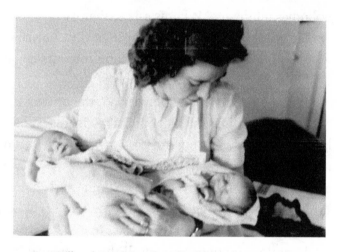

1948 Bill and Karola's twins Billy (lft.) and Margaret (rt.)

＊ ＊ ＊

Editor's Note:

Two years after the twins' birth, in 1950, they were diagnosed with polio, but with hospitalization and a required isolation period they recovered completely, with no side effects.

# CHAPTER 16

*Moving Again; Carolyn is Born*

**WE MOVED FROM MARLU FARMS** in September 1949 to Pleasantdale Farms in West Orange, New Jersey. We then had to move again in late 1952, this time to Uplands Farm in Cold Spring Harbor, Long Island, New York.

✳ ✳ ✳

Early spring 1953 found us still living on Uplands Farm. Bill was one of the dairymen there and his duties were to milk approximately twelve cows, clean out the barn, and tend to the calves in another barn.

The foreman, Joe Poullion, had just decided to have three milking sessions instead of two. This meant Bill's day would be mostly spent in the barn with hardly any rest or relief. These animals were all blue-ribbon stock with papers to prove it. Before doing the milking, Bill had to put on a white linen jumpsuit and wash each udder and tail with an Ivory soap solution, followed by a clear water rinse. This three-time milking plan did not sit well with him but it seemed a schedule that would not be easily altered.

Bill made up his mind that as soon as he found another job

we would move again, after only a number of months in Cold Spring Harbor. Matters became more pressing when I suspected I was pregnant. This suspicion was confirmed a month later by Dr. Wilbur, a doctor in Huntington, Long Island. Now we knew it was time to move. There was no room in the present accommodations for another baby. The twins had the smallest bedroom, not deserving that name at all. It housed two little beds and a tiny closet with barely room to allow passage. Another change Bill wanted to make was to not be a dairyman any longer. With the hard work and early hours, his hands began to suffer from rheumatism; he had had enough of sterilizing the milk bottles in hot water and using strong detergents. He wanted to pursue his real love, gardening.

1953 Karola and Bill

After a few trips to the city to the employment agency, nothing special had turned up. By chance an ad in the local paper advertised an opening for a gardener in Oyster Bay, which was not too far away from Cold Spring Harbor. Bill went for an interview with the superintendent, a Mr. Kealing, of the Appledore Estate, which was owned by H.P. Davison, a businessman on Wall Street. He got the job and seemed certain that the living accommodations would be satisfactory for our growing family. This was now the third time I had to move while pregnant and the fifth move since leaving Germany. As Bill had to work till the last possible hour in Cold Spring Harbor and at the first possible opportunity in Oyster Bay, the packing was left to me. Well, somehow, we made it. We spent a good summer in the new place; the twins had a little area to put in their own tiny garden and could even share a swing set and slide with the superintendent's granddaughter. Soon came enrollment period for the twins in the nearby school. The problem was that they would not have bus service because the distance to school was less than two miles, and Bill was not allowed to bring them or pick them up, since his boss did not want him to miss work. In addition, there was Highway 25A to cross. So, pregnant or not, I hiked the distance to and from school with them, until one day the regular routine resulted in a slight glitch. I got the kids to school on time but, exhausted, I promptly fainted. When the class teacher revived me and the school administration heard I had walked with the children daily, they were aghast that their father was prohibited from driving them to and from school. This was all due to the superintendent, Bill's boss. When Mr. and Mrs. Davison, the estate owners, heard about the situation they were incensed. They determined that Bill could bring the kids to school in the morning, and other help on the premises would be sent to pick them up in the afternoon. What a relief that was for me, along with feeling I no longer belonged to a lowly servant status.

An amusing occurrence was related to us by the person picking the kids up after school. This guy was easygoing and casually mannered, in his upper forties, and once while driving took out his upper dental plate, removed a food particle and put the dental plate back in. Billy stared at him in disbelief. "Hey, can you do that again?" he asked. But no go. For a while that was a major puzzlement to Billy and it took some time to explain the reality of false teeth.

*\* \* \**

Christmas came and went. I became definitely pregnant-looking and fatigued on a regular basis. The visits to Dr. Wilbur became more frequent until he said "Well, D-Day is near, probably around the twenty-first of February." Too bad it would not be February 16, my mother's birthday. Maybe then my parents would not think so harshly about a third child after twins. They thought our family was complete with a son and a daughter. Any additional child, in their minds, was just an added burden, another mouth to feed, not to mention the time and money spent rearing it. I felt sorry for their limited thinking. They had never been able to plan on having several children in their marriage. That was a difficult time in every way. Women could only endure one caesarean section then, which my birth was. A second one was considered a risk of death for the mother.

1950 Karola's parents' 28th anniversary

What a consolation that there was no need to give an explanation or account to anyone regarding my pregnancy. We wanted this child, our love created it, and we would certainly nurture it. Picking a name was not easy and it was already February. Should we have a daughter, we decided on Carolyn. If we had a boy, his name would be either John or Peter. Margaret and Billy also helped sort out names and they liked those. The two had been getting increasingly impatient. They seemed to suspect the whole thing was a fraud and there would be no new baby. But, there was Mom's big belly as evidence of a pending arrival. Sleeping was so uncomfortable and shifting from one side to the other was a laborious undertaking. Hauling myself up and down the stairs was another enervating venture. It seemed that the lively baby had shifted way down. I was getting sick of maternity clothes. The few I had were beginning to look seedy. There'd been too much washing and ironing of them. Would I ever look slim again? My hair looked such a mess, no matter what I did to it. Well, after payday I could get a permanent. Why did I feel so sorry for myself lately? I guess I couldn't really ever talk to my relatives. Gee, it would have been nice to visit my aunts and cousins. If they had just lived close by, they would have given me a party and spoiled me because of the expected baby and we could have talked about it on and on. When the twins came home from school, I was happy to have company again. Being alone so much was not good.

I was making each of them a new sweater. They saw me making little baby things and thought I didn't love them anymore. They were getting weary of our fussing about a person who didn't even exist yet, in their eyes. There was a crib, rocking chair, and dresser in a separate room, while they still had to share everything. I gather they didn't mind, though. They had been so used to it all their lives—even before being born.

We settled with our neighbors across the street, Peggy and Harry, that if I had to go to the hospital at night, they would take the twins for supper and overnight. Harry would drive them to school in the morning and pick them up in the afternoon. Marge and Billy couldn't wait for that to happen because they would be able to watch TV! We wouldn't get one, as they were too expensive. We could watch the new baby; it'd be much more fun. This was the first time the kids would be sleeping away from home. They packed their little suitcases to be ready for the big event.

Inge Simpson said that as soon as she got the news, she would come for a week or so to keep house until I felt stronger again. That was a huge help. I wouldn't have to worry about anything and it would be great to have company. And there would be someone else to admire the new baby! Bill's parents in Brooklyn didn't even know they would have another grandchild soon. For some of their dumb reasons we had not been on speaking terms for eight months. It seemed they had no real feelings. Watching other families, how close they were, could set me off on a marathon of self-pity. But that was bad for the baby. Instead, I baked some cookies before the kids and Bill got home and made a triple recipe to put some aside for when I had to go to the hospital. Keeping busy chased the gloomy thoughts away. The kitchen smelled good. All of a sudden there was this pain . . . a contraction? Ah, it was probably nothing; we could eat supper. Oops—there was the pain again. Better call the doctor. "Yes," he said, "time to get ready for the hospital."

Everybody got super excited. This was it! The kids were happy as larks to go to the neighbors. They even knew what was on TV that night! They took a big box of my sugar cookies along. Thank the Lord, no snow or icy roads; they were nice and clear. Too many long stoplights, though. The moon hung low, looking orange. I would feel better once I got to the hospital. I hoped I'd make it in time.

Finally, we arrived. My big entrance coincided with my water breaking. In spite of all the precautions, the overflow went onto the beautiful carpet in the lobby. This brought some immediate attention in the form of a wheelchair. I said goodbye to Bill and told him, "There is no sense for you to wait. We will call you with the news." We went up the elevator to the maternity floor and everyone was waiting there to get me ready.

"How many pregnancies?" the nurse asked.

"This is my second."

"How old is the other youngster at home?

"I have two children." She had a confused look on her face. "Oh, you have twins!"

The nurse was looking suspiciously at my abdomen. She started working faster to get me ready. "Ah, there is your doctor."

"Oh, we are sorry," said Dr. Wilbur. "There is no room available right now for any more women in labor. Everything is filled to capacity. Would you mind being parked in the hall?"

"Heck no," I told him, "nobody knows me here anyway."

The pains were coming strong and fast. Now we rolled to the delivery room.

"Bear down only when I tell you," Dr. Wilbur instructed. "Now. Breathe deep, and again, push now. Look up to the overhead mirror; we are seeing a nice head of hair. Nice going! You have a beautiful daughter!"

Carolyn let out some tiny wails.

"She has good lungs," the doctor said. "She should be a good singer."

I couldn't believe it was all over. What a glorious, happy feeling.

"Put the baby on my tummy so I can see her," I asked the nurse.

The nurse fussed over her, put drops in her eyes and an identification bracelet on her tiny wrist. The blanket was wrapped around protesting arms and legs, and then—there she was, lying right on top of my flat tummy. I meant to say, "Hey there," but I couldn't. I was speechless and ecstatic, floating on this wave of love and happiness, on February 17, 1954.

The doctor called Bill and at 8:30 he came to see his new baby girl. It was almost not worth going home, it happened so fast after all. Wonderful, glorious, perfect! Thank you, Lord!

This time around I only had to stay four days in the hospital. Inge had already arrived at our home. She visited me and little Carolyn at the hospital, too. It was such a comfort to me knowing that all was well at home. What a difference from my first time giving birth! Everything was so unknown then, and this time our undivided attention could go to just one baby.

Inge was a great cook and took over the hanging of the laundry, which saved me from navigating those stairs and carrying the heavy baskets. The baby diapers and the laundry were done separately, quite a difference from prior double loads. With Inge's help I could gain my former pep back much faster than if I had to do the home chores alone, given that Bill had to follow his own demanding job schedule.

While we lived in Cold Spring Harbor, Bill had joined the Huntington *Liederkranz* (German singing group). There he made many dear friends, among them Margaret and Conrad Buttner. They were truly excited about our new addition to the family. When we asked them to be godparents for Carolyn, they were absolutely thrilled. On Margaret and Billy's sixth birthday, baby Carolyn was baptized at St. Peter's Evangelical Lutheran Church in Huntington, Long Island by Reverend Paul H. Pallmeyer. All the Buttners' friends were so happy for them, especially since their own son, Robert, had no children. In a way this made them feel like grandparents. Afterward we invited Conrad and Margaret for a simple luncheon, so the seven of us enjoyed a cozy little party together. The twins had a fun time on that May 9, 1954, with the added benefit of ideal weather, warm and balmy. Bill and I were hoping the Buttners had a good time also and would not ask why no one else from our family had shown up. They really looked as if they were having a delightful Sunday.

1954 baby Carolyn and Bill, Karola, Billy, Margaret

I was so pleased that our third child was now baptized, too. It had worked out so well to have the Buttners as godparents. We still had not had a chance to be affiliated with any church, due to our assorted moves up to that point. During our stay at Cold Spring Harbor, I had been able to finally get my US Citizenship—after almost an entire year of tracking down two witnesses who could vouch for having known me for two full years, were not related, and were also US citizens. What a fantastic feeling to finally belong and not be a stateless person anymore, and to have all my children baptized. Yet, on that most wonderful baptismal day we had no film to load in our camera and the Buttners had forgotten theirs. Sadly, there are no pictures to mark that great occasion.

✳ ✳ ✳

Editor's Note:

Karola became a US Citizen in 1953. She recounted how after a harrowing interrogation at the court in Newark, New Jersey, she was informed that a swearing in of new citizens would be occurring in fifteen minutes and if she hurried, she could join them. Finally at the rank of a true American, she and Bill went to New York City to celebrate her new status at Café Hindenburg in the Yorkville section of Manhattan. En route the taxi was delayed in traffic, due to the German-American Steuben Parade, of all things. Bill did not have sufficient cash to pay the fare but offered the hand-painted tie he was wearing; the cab driver agreeably accepted.

# CHAPTER 17

*Another Move, Another Birth*

**IN 1956, AFTER THREE YEARS** living in Oyster Bay, we had to move again, only this time I was not pregnant. We relocated to Dogwood Hill, an estate owned by Mr. De Ganahl, in Navesink (near Red Bank), New Jersey. I worked part-time in the main house as the upstairs maid, laundress, and babysitter for Mr. De Ganahl's visiting grandchildren, nieces, and nephews. Bill was the gardener and caretaker and oversaw a comprehensive garden and peach orchard, along with the grounds. Bill's parents visited frequently and even stayed with the children when I flew to see my parents in 1957—the first time I had seen them since leaving Germany, and the last. As wonderful as it was in the summers, December 1960 through February 1961 was a particularly cold and harsh winter period. For some time, I had not felt very well, and my formerly punctual nature had forsaken me. Now and then the irregular bleeding made doctor visits necessary. My own thoughts were, *here I go into early menopause.* After all, I was soon to be thirty-nine the following December. Dr. Podell in Red Bank, who had delivered the twins, examined me and wanted to know about my daily work schedule. He looked very concerned and did some further tests. He gave me the diagnosis of a possible tumor and ordered strict bed rest. He told me to quit my job as a maid and come back in four weeks, and if anything bothered or worried me to give him a call.

That strict bed rest order was difficult to follow, not to mention the guilty feelings I had about all the extra tasks Bill had to do. He organized a schedule for Marge, Billy, and Carolyn regarding the helpful chores they could assume, according to their ages. At the same time, we had to tell Mr. and Mrs. De Ganahl of the situation. They were very understanding. I recommended Amelia Raeder, a friend from the Navesink Methodist Church, to cover my duties at the main house. She had been looking for a part-time job, so this suited her very well. The only issue was she did not drive. Enter Bill, the chauffeur, with car service for Amelia to and from Dogwood Hill.

After a long four weeks, a sore back, and not feeling energetic, I returned to Dr. Podell. "Well," he said, "I have a suspicion that you may be pregnant." I thought, thank God, no tumor. He went on to say, "But I cannot keep you as a patient, since times have changed. Everything nowadays is specialization. You have to see an obstetrician for your prenatal care. Congratulate Bill for me and here are the telephone numbers of doctors to contact." There were three of them, all in the same office. After my disappointment of not being able to stay with Dr. Podell, I immediately called these specialists and made an appointment. Next, I called Bill to pick me up and told him I had some interesting news.

In the car I had to tell him then and there about the exciting state of affairs. He almost drove off the road with the surprise and thrill of becoming a father once again. We made a pact to keep this to ourselves for a while, since I still had to take it easy and rest a lot. With this third pregnancy things could easily go wrong because of my age. It was fortunate we now had a small policy with Blue Cross & Blue Shield of New Jersey for hospital expenses but we were not covered for the approaching doctors' fees. We could arrange a payment plan, however; they were very accommodating and considerate of Bill's low income.

Two years earlier we had to deal with an onslaught of tonsillectomies and appendectomies (Billy and Carolyn) and needed to ask Mr. De Ganahl for a loan to pay the hospital and doctor bills. He was appalled at the cost of it all so he gave Bill a raise, with the stipulation he should enroll in Blue Cross. It was a blessing having such a great boss. Bill's parents in Brooklyn would not even consider offering a loan, and they were family.

My appointment with the new doctors went well. I received all kinds of uplifting pamphlets, information and, more importantly, was prescribed vitamin supplements to get my energy going again. To sit in a waiting room with all these expectant mothers was in one way quite a positive boost, but in another way intimidating because they all appeared far more well off than we were. But I was happily expecting another baby, so I concentrated on the primary issues and basic values close to our hearts. Eventually my strength came back, and I had to watch my diet. In those days the doctors did not allow much of a weight gain. They reasoned that it would make for a difficult delivery. Then came the day I could actually feel I had a live-in boarder kicking me! I felt well enough to sing in the choir again. On Mother's Day they had the custom of pinning white carnations on all the mothers' robes and a pink one on the robe of any expectant mother. Ha! That was my way of making the big announcement to the choir and congregation, but they had a hard time believing it. All eyes went to my stomach after taking the robe off and they could not see a thing. I had the tendency of hardly showing my pregnancies for a while and, well, they were not convinced until much later. This was also the right time to tell the De Ganahls, as well as the kids, that there would be a fourth baby coming sometime in November. Marge and Bill took the news quite agreeably, and Carolyn imagined this to be a new doll for her almost forgotten doll carriage. All three were so helpful, and that was an encouragement for me. The astonished and almost negative vibrations came from Bill's brother Johnny and his wife Heli, who had been living in Mount Kisco, and from Bill's parents, who were still living in Brooklyn. That summer our friend Inge Simpson went to Germany to visit our mutual hometown of Offenbach and she offered to tell my parents the good news. Personally, I did not like that idea but figured so what? I knew my father of all people would have something dumb to say anyway. Sure enough, when she was in Germany, she happened to bump into my father in one of the main department stores. After the astonishment of seeing each other, she gave him our greetings and relayed the news of my current pregnancy and his pending new grandchild. Oh my, poor Inge had to hear a *barrage* of outrage about my stupidity and bear the force of Niagara Falls pounding her thunderously and publicly in a major department store. She was devastated. She told him, "Herr Friedmann, my mother would be in seventh heaven if she would get such news, but I cannot have children. Be glad that they are all well and happy and supporting themselves." After she returned from her trip and had recovered somewhat from the shock of that encounter, she could muster a faint snicker about it but, for me, the sadness I felt from his reaction remained for a long time.

The summer months went quickly, and we were considering first names for a boy or girl. We narrowed it down to Peter and Louise or Dorothy. My friends from the choir and church were so delighted about my condition that I felt absolutely spoiled. Mr. and Mrs. De Ganahl gave me an early baby present: a clothes dryer so I would not have to lug all that wet laundry outside to hang on the line, and they also promised an eight-week diaper service once the baby was born. These amenities were coming my way for the first time and I began to feel how nice it was. At the end of a hot September day my feet were so swollen I felt like an inflated wet rag.

Bill said, "I'll take you now to choir practice."

I said, "Go and tell them I can't make it. I need to just put my feet up and relax."

"Well," he said, "Come along and I will go in and tell them. Then we'll go right back home."

The man was very persuasive, so I agreed and went along. Once there he said, "Since you're here, you might as well go in and tell them yourself." I thought to myself, *What gives?*

I dragged myself in and heard an eruption of shouting. "Surprise! This is your baby shower!"

I could not begin to believe it. The entire room was filled with ladies. There was a big table overflowing with presents, most of them handmade, a beautiful cake, a bowl filled with, yes, pink punch. The centerpiece was something I had never seen before: a deep bowl sprouting several branches hung with eggshells halved lengthwise that formed cradles, each filled with pastel tulle and a teeny, tiny baby doll swinging on pastel ribbons from the branches. I was so stunned and surprised I had to sit down and cry for a bit. Besides being upset that nobody had given me a hint so I could spruce myself up, I must have looked a teary sight. Kleenex time!

It turned out to be a beautiful evening, after all. Someone had even brought a camera and took pictures. Sadly, they could not be developed properly because there was insufficient lighting or something to that effect. It was such a loss that I could not put this memory in an album.

At the end of October, I wondered how I could go another day with this pregnancy. It got to be so exhausting and my feet by then could only fit into Bill's old slippers. At night when lying down I could not get into a comfortable position because we also needed a new mattress. I was unable to escape the valley that had been burrowed by prolonged use and kept sinking into the middle. It was not possible to turn on my side or sleep on my back. I had heard the expression *false labor* but did not believe in such a thing. Yet it did not spare me. I woke up in the middle of the night with contractions ten minutes apart. I thought, *Do I call the doctor now, or wake up Bill to take me to the hospital?* I paced the floor and moaned, thinking maybe it would go away. Then after some time I felt nothing. This scenario repeated itself on following evenings.

I had to tell the doctor how worn out I felt because no rest was foreseeable. He said, "You are having false labor." It went on and on till about November 14. I couldn't take it anymore. I spoke with the doctor and he said to come in for an exam. He said, "This baby is ready to be born. We want to spare you any more of this agony, so you pick a day for delivery." So, pick a day I did, and Friday, November 17 seemed like a good date.

The doctor gave me some sleeping pills to last through the night of the sixteenth and said, "If you wake up during the night you know you are in *real labor*. Have some nights of good sleep and we will see you at Riverview Hospital on Friday morning at eight o'clock, unless this baby decides otherwise."

I was punctual in reporting to the Riverview maternity floor on the seventeenth. The nurses took over with all kinds of probes and tests, and they initiated the labor process. They showed me to a small room where I could be in repose, meditate on waiting for contractions to start, and time them. Occasionally, a nurse poked her head in to ask how I was doing.

"Just fine," I said for most of the day. I was supposed to be a pro at this. Ha!

I had no concept of time. At one point when the nurse showed up, I told her to hurry up and get this body into the delivery room! Everybody seemed to be ready.

The doctor told me, "Just a few pushes will do. And take a

look in the overhead mirror. You can see your baby coming."

It was a girl. She was so beautiful. While the nurses did their routine of putting the identification bracelet on the baby, etc., I looked out the window and it felt like a new soul from God had entered the room, right out of the blue sky. It was the most profound feeling.

Now I was wheeled to my semi-private room. I asked the nurse to call home with the grand news: "We have a Dorothy Louise here." I hope Billy was not too disappointed it wasn't a little brother. The nurse came back saying, "Your husband will come later during visiting hours and your son says, "If she is pretty, we'll keep the little sister." Everybody was euphoric.

The doctor came in to congratulate me and said, "All is fine with your new daughter and I have signed you over to the pediatrician." Another change of doctors? I had never heard of so many changes. I had thought we could all go to Dr. Podell again. No such luck. This was now the age of specialization. But I wanted to keep floating on this happy cloud and give my full attention to our new baby. I could stay in the hospital an entire week and learn the new methods of baby care that had evolved since the last birth. My, how things had changed! I guess it was all for the better, like the way Riverview Hospital had modernized since the time the twins were born. At that time, it was like a little private villa with inn-like awnings and a water view. By now it had become a huge, industrial hospital complex with the very latest equipment and procedures. I would let myself and little Dorothy be spoiled while we were there.

The following week would be Thanksgiving. I would be in the hospital until Friday. Bill and the children would have to go out for their turkey dinner, but I didn't feel guilty. No, not me. I was so thrilled and grateful that all was well. We were now a sextet—wow!

✳ ✳ ✳

During the next few days, I could really get to know this cuddly new little daughter of mine. I loved to draw out the feeding time— afterward the babies were so quickly collected and taken back to the nursery. Bill managed to come every day during evening visiting hours and brought me lots of fresh fruit, including Golden Delicious apples. I don't know why but I had such a craving for this variety that I just gobbled them up.

On the evening before Thanksgiving another woman was rushed into my room. The dividing curtain was drawn but I overheard the drama.

This unfortunate woman had been in an automobile accident but seemed only slightly hurt at first. Then she went into an early labor. She was only seven months pregnant and had to have a caesarean section. She delivered a little boy. The father came to his wife's bedside and broke the news gently that the baby was not doing well, and he summoned the priest to have an emergency baptism. These developments were happening so fast. The priest had just baptized the baby when it died before it could get the last rites. The parents, the doctors, and the priest were all in shock. By now I was in tears and could not fathom how closely death could follow birth.

The atmosphere in the room was dense with these solemn emotions of trauma, a short-lived joy about the birth, then sadness upon sadness. There was absolutely nothing one could say or do, just pray for that family. It was so unfair that the next day was Thanksgiving, the day of giving thanks. Our meals were served, and I could not subdue a feeling of guilt for having a beautiful, healthy daughter, and this lady had to leave the hospital with empty arms after she herself had barely recovered from her physical ordeal. It was not possible for her to be moved to another room as there was no space available. She had to witness the opposite of what had happened to her, with the nurse bringing little Dorothy for her feedings. Bill, the happy new dad, would only talk very quietly, respecting the enormous grief this other family had to endure.

That Saturday I was released from the hospital. Passing by the cashier's office (here comes the bill), all we had to remit was one dollar for the use of the telephone. Hard to believe, but that was it. How wonderful to have health insurance!

Coming home with a new baby was ecstasy. A bassinet was set up in our bedroom and all was ready. The kids couldn't believe how small babies were. Right away Carolyn wanted to bring out the doll carriage, but this was postponed for a while. Everybody wanted to hold this tiny bundle. How wonderful! For the next two weeks we had engaged Amelia Raeder's sister, just to come in for a couple of hours in the morning or early afternoon. That was mainly to have some company, so I would not succumb to postpartum blues, as happened twice before and almost sent me into deep depression. It is amazing how nature works. Fluctuating emotions can unhinge a person quite easily.

For my own checkups I had to go to the gynecologist; for Dorothy it was the pediatrician. The rest of the clan could again see Dr. Podell. He was so happy that everything had gone well for us.

The support of everyone in the family, plus having the comfort of Amelia's sister visiting, was immensely reassuring. Missing sleep was the only serious drawback with an infant at hand, but once Dorothy slept through the night it was better. I made it a rule during the day to nap whenever the baby did, but I guess one ear was always on guard. Many times I wished I could be more relaxed and easygoing, but I could not shake the hyper-consciousness and overriding sense of responsibility of being a new mother again. We had been planning Dorothy's baptism and did not want to wait too long to do it. One month after coming into the world she was baptized on Sunday, December 17, 1961, at the Navesink Methodist Church by Reverend Richard Hoye, the youngest minister we had ever had at this church. He had been visiting us to see the new addition to the Schuette clan and was looking forward to the event.

Saturday, the sixteenth, it started snowing and then on top of that, sleet! We were very worried how to get ourselves and the baby paraphernalia, warm baby bottle, blankets, etc., safely to church. Alvira, who lived across from the church, called us and said that everything would be shoveled, sanded, and red-carpeted up into church by Sunday morning, so there would be no danger of slipping or falling with our precious cargo, as long as we pulled up right to the carpet! This was truly *red-carpet* treatment! We were so touched. At this time there was already a Christmas service, with a beautifully decorated tree near the altar. All my choir friends beamed as we came in and took our seats in the front row. The entire congregation had been anticipating this occasion. It was so appropriate, an infant baptized at the Christmas service. It was moving and beautiful.

Bill's parents had not come from Brooklyn, nor had Johnny and Heli. They never took part in any church services where the children were concerned. As disappointing as this was, it made things easy for us not having to put them up, given that there was no room. I also did not have to deal with feeding the *Krauts*, who were always difficult to please. It would have been a big stress on the budget, too. Now, after church we could all just relax. The ladies from the church had sent over casseroles and other thoughtfully prepared dishes. What a loving bunch. And now there was a new Christian in our midst. Christmas was coming and it was truly a joyful one. Mr. and Mrs. De Ganahl were so generous in giving us a huge food basket and expressing sincere congratulations on our new daughter. The emotional connection of people admiring one's new baby is a grand gift for a mother, who tends never to forget it. Even the infant absorbs this warmth and caring—at least I believe that.

1962 Carolyn and baby Dorothy

Editor's Note:

Only two years after Dorothy's birth in 1961 it was moving time again, from Red Bank, New Jersey to Fair Haven, New Jersey. In 1966, as Margaret headed to college and twin Bill enlisted in the Air Force, their youngest sister entered Kindergarten. After only three years there, it felt like no sooner were schedules and routines adjusted than the remaining household was uprooted yet again—to New Canaan, Connecticut, known as *The Next Station to Heaven*. The family lived there for fifteen years. With roots firmly planted, Karola worked at an insurance company and a local bank. She and Bill saw daughter Carolyn off to college, celebrated their twenty-fifth wedding anniversary, and experienced an empty nest after Dorothy's acceptance to college. Highlights of ensuing years included the marriage of Carolyn and the birth of two grandchildren, Michael and David. During the year David was born, 1984, Bill retired and moved with Karola to their first rental apartment in Norwalk, Connecticut. This was the only time in their married life that they did not live in a gardener's cottage provided by the employer. Retirement for Bill did not last long, however. He passed away suddenly in June of 1986, on his sixty-eighth birthday.

1972 Bill and Karola's 25th anniversary

# CHAPTER 18

## *Catherine, the Sister I Never Had*

**"MY NAME IS CATHERINE KENNEDY,"** she said, standing in front of my desk, looking at me like I should know who she was.

"May I help you?" I replied.

"Well, I just want to pick up my mother."

Seeing no one in the lobby, I said, "Who is your mother?"

"It's Mrs. Greer, she must have been here to see you."

I knew the name, she had just left through the other door, after she had refused my offer to guide her down the stairs. Now here was Mrs. Greer's daughter. Mrs. Greer was the lady who always brought her British pension checks for me to exchange into dollars and who volunteered at the thrift shop in town and always brought me some left-over wool (she knew I was a knitter), or another cross-stitch kit someone had grown tired of and the shop could not sell. These thrift items never went to waste and many a sweater or afghan was fashioned for my family. We always talked about needlework, as she was a weaver. Over the years she stopped driving and I noticed her eyesight was beginning to fail. Proud as she was, she would not accept my assistance navigating the steps. She had never mentioned any family. So, this was her daughter, Catherine Kennedy.

Losing Bill, I had become a widow in 1986. Soon thereafter, Catherine started working part-time at our bank branch of what was then Union Trust Company. Through our daily contact we became closer and shared many a conversation about family and other topics. Before we knew it, a deep friendship had blossomed. For me, she became the sister I never had. Both of us coming from Europe—she from Scotland—provided another basis for similar sensibilities, understanding, and, yes, an appreciation of different disciplines from the ones fading away in this country.

By and by we had daily talks on the phone and went out for occasional lunches. Eventually I got to meet some of her family. I belonged to the employee's club at the bank, and they offered periodic trips to Broadway shows and other events. We saw the Christmas show at Radio City Music Hall. She travelled with me as my guest on many a weekend bus trip: Lake Sunapee in New Hampshire, Twin Lighthouse in Gloucester, Massachusetts, and Montauk, Long Island. Whenever I received benefits involving shows or trips for two, Catherine happily joined me. A performance at the Goodspeed Opera House in Connecticut, including a night at a bed and breakfast, was among the varied ventures. The Bed and Breakfast Inn featured genuine old-fashioned décor; one felt like a member of the owner's extended family. In our room we had the old high beds with down comforters, along with additional accoutrements reminding us of yesteryear. Catherine's bed, however, was so high she needed to climb up onto it with the aid of a chair. Giggles and laughter ensued from this necessity, along with the anticipation of navigating during a nighttime nature call. But we had come prepared with flashlights and practiced the escape route forward and backward in advance, practical as we were. The show at the opera house was *Anything Goes*. A member of the Gershwin family was in the audience, generating a very stimulating and congested intermission.

After meeting and visiting Isa, a close cousin of Catherine who lived in Rhode Island, I was introduced to the game of Scrabble. My goodness, how intimidating it was. They had lots of experience playing and were such experts at the game. I felt like the dumbest greenhorn! Catherine reassured me otherwise, as she was ever so kind. After a long time, I finally came to enjoy this game and even looked forward to it; we used to play at least once a week. Her dear friend Miriam from New York was sometimes able to visit just to play Scrabble. The interaction, conversation, and just being together provided an absolutely fun time.

The sequence of my memories of Catherine is not in order, but the memories are surely there. There wasn't a thing we didn't discuss! From commercials, politics, personal feelings, people we knew, what to do in a tricky or challenging situation, and what do you think about this or what do you think about that? Many a time we both came to the conclusion that we had definitely saved a fortune by not having to consult a psychologist. We seemed to always find help, inspiration, and knowledge from each other's experience. But where was that money we had obviously saved?

The shopping trips to Bradley's (which is no longer in business) always worked out in her favor. She made the sale deadline and had a coupon or a senior discount. I just could never quite beat that, and heaven knows I tried. By being a large or even an extra-large size, my choices were not as plentiful compared to her petite size. She had more to choose from, particularly at sale occasions. She called herself *vertically challenged*, which caused many a saleslady to chuckle.

Who came along for every important, larger purchase I made? Catherine. Her advice and input were so valuable, especially when I bought my own car. Bill and I had always bought used cars and driven them into the ground, so to speak. Being by myself now and unsure how to proceed, I felt I had no one to lean on for a definitive decision. On my own I decided, after some sleepless nights, to buy a *new* car. Catherine went with me and helped with finding the car for me. Thereafter she called it *our car* and drove it many times on our trips. When I still lived in Norwalk, she had a key to my place, and while I was at work in the bank, she wallpapered my bedroom. She was a lady of great talent and kindness. Her son, Ronald, later painted my living room. So many great deeds from the Kennedy clan!

After her sweet black dog passed away, I remember her coming into the bank with a tiny something wrapped in a blanket . . . it happened to be Suzie, her new little puppy. What a cutie! And how quickly she grew into a big dog!

Animals were Catherine's devotion: feeding the birds, boarding other people's pets for a day or longer; and rescuing a lost baby raccoon, naming it Jessie, and nursing it along lovingly. Later she had to release it back to its own world but missed it fiercely. We said many times, "I wonder how Jessie is doing!"

The daily consistency of our relationship was challenged suddenly by Catherine's decision to move to Narragansett, to be near the water, the *negative ions*, as she called it. A local agent scouted property agents there, and then came the time to visit locations and make a choice. Catherine asked me to come along and with a heavy heart I went, wondering why on earth she would want to move away from New Canaan. Selfish me, I was worried I would lose my best friend. Somehow it was like the bottom had fallen out from under me. Yet if it made my friend happy, I would just have to just deal with it. Catherine courted her Narragansett dream for quite a while and finally decided on a place she liked. Jean and Charlie, a couple of her friends from Scotland, came to visit and went with her to see the chosen house. They were baffled as to why she would want to leave New Canaan, her comfortable home, friends, and familiar neighborhood; they were simply dumbfounded.

Their conversations with her on the subject ultimately resulted in a change of heart. It had taken friends from outside the country to point to the blessings nearby. I was so happy about not losing my buddy, my friend, and my confidante. Most important, her decision had not been influenced by me. Many months after all this Catherine began to wonder herself why she had wanted a place in Narragansett. And years later the subject was forgotten while I still glowed from not having to say goodbye.

Eventually the moment came when my hope to move back to New Canaan from Norwalk led to actual possibility. The former Saxe Junior High School on South Avenue was on the agenda for years to be converted into affordable housing for the elderly, with unsuccessful results. Ultimately, the right people were in the right place, the circumstances were favorable, and by winter 1991 ground was broken (albeit deeply frozen) for what was to become Schoolhouse Apartments.

During our daily morning phone calls Catherine would read both of our horoscopes and, eerie as it seemed, mine always pointed to a great outcome: my relocation to New Canaan. In later years we wished we had kept those predictions, as it was all so uncanny. Now instead of Catherine moving away I finally moved back to New Canaan, and she came with me when I signed the lease. The day after Thanksgiving 1992, I was escorted to my own, new apartment and we celebrated with a cold bottle of ginger ale. Hurrah!

Now that I could actually plan for the move I had to get in gear and downsize; my new place was much smaller, but those were happy decisions. Ah, Christmas 1992. I was so happy to be in New Canaan again.

An amazing thing about Catherine and me was that we never ran out of meaningful conversation, as happens with some acquaintances. After the *how are you?* and mentioning the weather, one could be really stuck about the very next sentence.

Not so with us. A particularly favorite subject of ours to ponder was that if all the politicians around the world would only listen to us, we could straighten out those in power and peace would be at hand, according to *our* recipe! Too bad that never happened. And now that Catherine is no longer in *this world*, having departed in March 2002, she may have a much bigger influence in the company of so many philosophers and great statesmen up yonder. Scrabble and crossword puzzles may be small stuff to those in the beyond. It is my hope that Catherine will persuade the angels and archangels to nudge earthlings to reroute their brains and hearts to improve conditions around the globe. I am sure she will see to that.

Will we meet up there again? That happened to be frequent subject matter between us. She had an amusing expression for death: *when I snuff it*. We'd wonder if we would bump into each other wherever we would be. We admonished and reminded ourselves to be sure to leave instructions for our families, as we spent our time living in the moment. And Catherine could come up with the funniest jokes about final matters; but we would be writing those instructions sometime soon. We found it comforting letting each other know, in our way, about deeper feelings and messages within.

On one of our trips to Long Island by ferry from Bridgeport to Port Jefferson, Catherine's friend Miriam came along, and talk somehow snuck in about our *finals*. If you knew Miriam, she was always eager to tell a joke. But Catherine had to interject her own vignette about two friends attending a wake held for one of their buddies who had suddenly passed:

"So, did you notice how well he looked laid out in that coffin?" one friend asked.

"Yes, I noticed, but he should look great, he just returned from a two-week vacation!"

Such was the merriment of three mature ladies on an outing.

My treasure of memories may sound silly to others, but deep remembering is a soothing salve for the pain of missing her. The many shared moments keep her close. I know she is looking down on us smiling and, knowing her, will arrange a big welcome, a cup of tea, a Scrabble board, and paper and pencil to keep score. So, Catherine, *I'll be seeing you in all the old familiar places* . . .

# CHAPTER 19

### *"How to Stay Young"*

**I AM WRITING THIS ON** September 26, 2006. Several days ago, I went through albums from a while back to check what I could complete or arrange better. While looking at old postcards, some sent by Bill's Oma from Germany, I came across one I am sure I had not noticed before.

It was one of those moments I felt there was a little fairy dust in the air. On the back of the card, I saw Bill's handwriting, ever so tiny. I was awestruck by the message, knowing that whenever he read something of great meaning to him, he would write it down.

Still mystified that I had not discovered it while previously arranging the album, I could feel Bill grinning as he put a *fast one* over on me, after all this time.

I thought it appropriate to include the prose poem with my own reflections; it felt like my dear Bill was continuing to communicate with us by delivering this poignant message. "How to Stay Young," by Samuel Ullman, remains an ageless reflection.

Tomorrow will be two years since young Bill passed. Were my two Bills conspiring to have me discover the postcard? I shall never know while here on earth.

*pessimism - cynicism*

"How to Stay Young"

"How to Stay Young"
By Samuel Ullman

Youth is not a time of life. It is a state of mind; it is a temper of the will, a quality of the imagination, a vigor of the emotions, a predominance of courage over timidity, of the appetite for adventure over love of ease.

Nobody grows old by merely living a number of years; people grow old only by deserting their ideals. Years wrinkle the skin, but to give up enthusiasm wrinkles the soul. Worry, doubt, self-distrust, fear and despair—these are the long, long years that bow the head and turn the growing spirit back to dust.

Whether seventy or sixteen there is in every being's heart the love for wonder, the sweet amazement at the stars and the starlike things and thoughts, the undaunted challenge of events, the unfailing childlike appetite for *what next*, and the joy and the game of life.

You are as young as your faith, as old as your doubt; as young as your self-confidence, as old as your fear; as young as your hope, as old as your despair.

So long as your heart receives messages of beauty, cheer, courage, grandeur, and power from the earth, from man or from the Infinite, so long you are young.

1957 Karola and Bill's 10th anniversary

1997 Karola's 75th birthday and 50th anniversary arriving in America

# EPILOGUE

"The Receptionist I Most Admire"
Karola M. Schuette
Published in the May/June 1984 issue of *Topics*, an employee
publication of Union Trust Company.

*Reception—defined in the dictionary as: during a ceremonial occasion, where visitors or guests are personally welcomed, announced, and/or greeted.*

To start listing the many qualities a receptionist should have makes it immediately clear that, for this particular job, all these qualities become a necessity. It means to be punctual and on the job in order to meet and greet people— dependability. Proper attire, manners, and deportment are essential —cordiality. Good judgment and understanding are very helpful, too, and most of all, a receptionist needs awareness that he or she is a representative of the employer. When I started at U.T.C. it was at the reception desk. I still feel today it is a most important contact job.

But . . . I really wanted to talk about the one I most admire—the receptionist I never forgot.

Yes, she was on the job—always and foremost reliable, steadfast, impressive, friendly, truthful, and patient. With a kind, welcome and ever-guiding presence, her manner inspired confidence, yes, even reverence. One can look up to her in awe and have respect for her dedication. She knows about responsibility to and for all the people she meets. I first happened to come into her presence some 36 years ago and, at the time, was so impressed I was overcome with tears. In fact, I believe no one that meets her can come away without being profoundly moved.

These days she is not feeling too well but does not want to hear about retirement. After all, the test results and examinations showed nothing but natural causes contributing to her discomfort. There will be no retirement for her when the condition can be cured. Oh yes, she is still on the job. Day in, day out, in all kinds of weather, she is at her post. What an inspirational existence.

She is wearing a body brace for support now, until all that ails her has been healed. I think of her so often now in her time of trials and treatment and wish I could do something special in return for the inspiration she gives—still gives . . .

She will have a special birthday in 1986. Her age? One hundred years old—and proud of it. There will be a big party in her honor. She plans to be on the job that day, too, just like on any other day. And she hopes to be in good and shining health—no more body braces then . . .

Originating from France, she could not find a permanent residence at first here. It took a number of years and the help of many people before she could settle down to a permanent base from which she still receives and welcomes many visitors and many admirers. I, for one, belong to the latter and I am saluting this great lady now and particularly on her 100th birthday to come. My most admired receptionist. May she shine forth for many centuries to come, she that welcomes and receives so many . . . as so many years ago she welcomed and received me . . .

The following is an excerpt from the poem "The New Colossus" by Emma Lazarus.

Give me your tired, your poor,

Your huddled masses yearning to breathe free,

The wretched refuse of your teeming shore

Send these, the homeless, tempest-tossed to me.

I lift my lamp beside the golden door!

# ACKNOWLEDGMENTS...

## *and a Little Bit of History*

**MOM WAS THOROUGH IN HER** thinking. Early in the writing process she anticipated details and parts of a book beyond its story content, especially when it came to recognizing others. She was grateful to anyone who encouraged or cultivated any iota of her penned project. In addition, she felt indebted to those who sustained her health and fortified her spirit along the way.

The acknowledgments below begin with those of the author, Karola herself. They are followed by mine (Margaret), as editor, along with additional highlights reflecting both the developmental process and timeline of *Journey Between Two Worlds*.

First and foremost, Karola wanted to thank her family, without whom much of the storyline would be missing. Their unfolding lives emanating from her hopeless beginnings fed her desire to clarify her heritage and leave behind a legacy. To that end, each loved one received a copy of Karola's original three-ring binder version and can now augment it with the published edition.

Numerous friends and acquaintances buoyed her with support for her endeavor. One fundamental cheerleader to her process was a friend and director of programming at the New Canaan Library at the time, Cynde Bloom Lahey, currently at the Norwalk Public Library. Reading Karola's memoir, available only as typed pages from an old word processor, she recognized the potential for a published book and took the initial step of preservation: transcribing the words into a computer.

A technological overhaul was soon beginning at Schoolhouse Apartments, where Karola lived in New Canaan, and she was about to learn new skills for herself. Her friend and technical wizard Jack Messert was instrumental to the installment of updated equipment at the residence and launched her in a digital direction. She would often sweeten their sessions with Lindt's Lindor truffles for Jack as a token of appreciation.

For spiritual bonding and companionship, she thrived on visits with Nancy Pullins, who extended endless warmth and selfless generosity. In Ruth Borgman she found not only a kindred spirit and poetic soul but also a Shiatsu guru to soothe her physical ailments, forging a friendship of body and mind. Both Nancy and Ruth have joined Karola in the afterworld and, no doubt, are continuing an abiding friendship.

Adding to this support was her steadfast friend Catherine Kennedy, a soul sister. She and Karola spoke first thing every morning and solved all the world's problems with a stroke of humor and common-sense philosophy. Catherine was a frisky friend, commiserating rascal, and staunch Scottish pillar through thick and thin for her eternal pal. She now, too, is with Nancy, Ruth, and Karola. And, knowing Catherine, she's got a wickedly winning game of Scrabble going with them.

As a virtual den mother at Schoolhouse Apartments, Karola was as appreciative of her neighbors and service providers as they were of her. High on her list of thanks would be for the Getabout, the reliable local transportation service for the residents of Schoolhouse. They demonstrated their own appreciation by dubbing Karola their best customer. Her circle of support for the memoir (and beyond) knew no bounds. It radiated out to the entire arena in which she navigated. That circle included former bank colleagues, members of the Congregational Church and choir, and staff and visitors at New Canaan Library, where she volunteered her notary services with friendly charm. Another validating group was her book club. It met once a month to share literary insights with one another, along with newsworthy town tidbits. Toward the end of her life, when she felt the deadline of time bearing down, she verbalized to her medical team in New Canaan and at Norwalk Hospital her desire for them to receive a copy of her written story when all phases were completed. Surrounding that sentiment was her deep appreciation for their professionalism and human kindness, which kept her afloat. During her later stages of life's journey at Waveny Care Center, she maintained her inner drive to see the manifestation of her legacy. She shared outwardly and inwardly her endless thanks to all who propelled her toward that end. Her goal has mercifully been accomplished and will live on.

I hear Mom's voice in my head telling me there are more people to thank on her behalf. That may well be true, and I apologize to those not specifically named here. To be honest, Karola would thank everyone listed in her Rolodex. Blessings, all.

※ ※ ※

As for me, the editor, I remain awed by the magnanimity of Karola, my author mother. She is the indomitable, humble heroine who lived the life, then re-lived it so poignantly in *Journey Between Two Worlds*. If not for her, there would be no story, no me, no family, no nothing herein. Recording her memories was a difficult and stuttering start. But once she took off, it was satisfying to hear her occasionally refer to herself as being *in the zone*. Her long process brought me closer to her reality and inner realm. An extension to her story includes diary entries of my father, her beloved Bill. They add to the narrative and give a fuller picture of my parents' upbringing and who they were. I revel in the thought that *Journey Between Two Worlds* reflects not only my mother's life venture, but also a good slice of my father's journey. My thanks and love forever to both Mom and Dad.

After the passing of Karola in 2013 it took a while to resume the *Mom project*. With busy schedules, life meanderings, and Murphy's Law interruptions, the continuity fell into spasmodic mode. Meanwhile, guilt had crept in big time. A promise to a mother must not go unheeded, and the clock kept ticking. Then the impetus picked up with scanning, re-typing, and further digitizing. The hunt for literary services commenced in earnest. So did the frustrations. No source seemed right, for many reasons. Most were located in other states and that required mailing to unknown hinterlands. The very idea was abhorrent. It was like sending your underage, only child unescorted on an airplane to an unsupervised destination. Unthinkable!

A different avenue: cold calls to typing services in my own city. That's when I struck gold. On a sunny day on my late father's birthdate, I reached a pleasant person named Karen Wilder of Wilder's Word Processing, right in my own neighborhood. She actually made an appointment with me to see the work—in person! No mailing! It felt like I was bringing my offspring on opening day to a special childcare center! And I was. This lead up to Karen is necessary to convey the good fortune aligning that day to rescue Mom's disassembled chapters. Karen Wilder was my lifeline to setting *Journey Between Two Worlds* on course. She was its devoted caretaker and nurturer, applying her professional efficiency and developmental guidance. Moreover, she was a consistently calming, encouraging influence in word and demeanor. Quite frankly, it does not seem possible that the memoir could have reached fruition without her. The beloved child, *Journey Between Two Worlds,* grew up and graduated because of Karen Wilder.

More work lay ahead, particularly editing, which required undivided attention... and much of it. With intervening activities time became scarce. Then in 2020 came COVID-19 and sheltering-in and, yes, time. It afforded uninterrupted concentration to tackle editing head-on and bring the manuscript to readiness.

As a result, the moment arrived for a family member to review a final version. I could always count on my sister, Carolyn, to give her honest opinions and thoughts. I value her sisterly insights and overall contribution to this personal enterprise.

My dear friends have lifted me up throughout the entire process. Their validation and positivity fortified my confidence and ability to plow ahead boldly with the work required. Their enduring love and care, as well as their invigorating humor, supplemented my wellbeing like daily vitamins.

I am indebted to Christopher Porterfield for his most generous and professional editing suggestions and contributions. His consummate expertise from years as an editor at Time Magazine, along with our lengthy neighborly and friendship status, have contributed immeasurably to an assured development of the text. My deepest gratitude to you, Chris.

Ilana Golin brought precise editing skills to select ancillary parts of *Journey Between Two Worlds.* I am grateful for her clarity and perception of verbal intention.

I thank Marcia Pally for her enthusiastic endorsement of my editing and publishing determination. She is not only a friend, but also an author who knows a thing or two about writing books, having written thirteen (!). Marcia also assisted with recommendations and resources. One invaluable referral was Barbara Shulman, who generously extended her legal services.

A big hurdle was finding a publisher. Researching them took a long time and none were right. I held the manuscript close.

Then another serendipitous moment occurred...through Karen again. She had been working with an author client whose book had just been published. Impressed with the quality of the end result, she suggested I reach out to his publisher. It couldn't hurt. Before doing so, it seemed a good idea to speak with this client to gather first-hand impressions of his publishing experience. All stellar. With his encouragement I reached out. Thank you, Charles Gomez, and congratulations on your award-winning autobiography, *Cuban Son Rising*. Your publisher, Koehler Books, became my publisher!

My gratitude to John Koehler, of Koehler Books, stretches to the moon and back. Accepting the manuscript and Karola's story seemed inspired by divine intervention, and our tenacious author is undoubtedly basking in celestial delirium. I thank my editor, Becky Hilliker, and the Koehler team for their professionalism and personable approach that enables the human element to shine through.

Danielle Koehler, of Dalitopia Media and Koehler Books, has skills and creative imagination that are distinctly evident on the website and cover for *Journey Between Two Worlds*. I am grateful for her sensitivity to the desired vision and detail of each, and for her dedicated fine tuning.

On the social media front I have Julien Frei to acknowledge for initially setting me up on Facebook, a critical avenue for promotion. Though technical dexterity is only one aspect of his multiple talents, it catapulted me to the starting line of media engagement.

Melissa Dybwad (UniversalByDesign.com) provided expanded services and continued guidance in the media and marketing domain; she is someone I'd be lost without. Upon our first Zoom meeting I knew she was a special find, and that has proven itself ever since. Her work ethic, promotional ideas and creativity, passion for her projects, and warm humanity are laudable attributes that will stimulate the marketing of *Journey Between Two Worlds*.

My long-term friend Laura Engel from early college days, who remains a bosom buddy and avid reader, read Karola's memoir a long time ago when it was in its heavy three-ring binder stage. Laura has been my champion throughout life. Upon hearing I found a publisher she sent a card kept for almost two decades until the right recipient (me!) and moment came into view. On the card is a lady in fine form taking a swan dive off a high board, with a John Burroughs declaration: *Leap and the net will appear*. Indeed.

Margaret Schuette
Editor

CPSIA information can be obtained
at www.ICGtesting.com
Printed in the USA
LVHW052309130721
692559LV00001B/32